JESUS, SET ME FREE!

INNER FREEDOM THROUGH CONTEMPLATION

by

GEORGE A. MALONEY, S.J.

DIMENSION BOOKS
DENVILLE, NEW JERSEY

Imprimi Potest:
Rev. Eamon Taylor, S.J.
Provincial of the New York Province
August 18, 1977

—DEDICATION—

To my four brothers, Emmons,
Denis, Vern and Clayton Maloney,
that the Lord may gift them with
a continued grace of inner freedom.

ACKNOWLEDGEMENTS

Sincere thanks to Sister Joseph Agnes of the Sisters of
Charity of Halifax for reading and typing this manuscript.
Grateful acknowledgement is made to the following
publishers: Darton, Longman & Todd, Ltd., and
Doubleday & Company, Inc., N.Y. for excerpts from *The
Jerusalem Bible,* copyright 1966 by Darton, Longman &
Todd, Ltd., and Doubleday and Company, Inc. All
scriptural texts are from *The Jerusalem Bible* unless
otherwise noted. To the magazine: *Catholic Charismatic*
for permission to use ideas expressed in an article entitled
"The Spiritual Life Demands Discipline" (Vol. 1, no. 3,
1976; pp. 36-41.)

TABLE OF CONTENTS

INTRODUCTION

You and I are more slaves than freed persons. Part of our slavery consists in having forgotten what true freedom means as children of God. We often are content to live in the narrow confines of our slavery, mainly because everyone else is in the same prison. Blindness is not so great a suffering if all human beings were born blind and never could know any other possibility. But blindness would become unbearable if there were among all blind persons one man who really could see!

The way we perceive ourselves, God and the world is fairly much the same way others perceive the same relationships. That precisely is part of our slavery. But Jesus Christ came among us with the eyes of God. He was "the true light that enlightens all men" (Jn 1:9). That light shines in our darkness and cannot be overpowered by our darkness (Jn 1:5).

To illustrate the power of Jesus Christ to set us free, I have chosen the traditional Byzantine icon of Jesus raising Lazarus from the dead. His friend, Lazarus, had been dead and in the tomb for four days before Jesus stood before that tomb. Jesus weeps because He cares! He enjoys the fullness of life. He comes to give us a share in that fullness (Jn 10:10).

Yet like Lazarus, how we live in the confinement of our own dark selfishness. We are not alive to God's truth. We are bound in so many ways. Yet to all who wish, Jesus can

5

say those same words addressed to the dead Lazarus: "Unbind him, let him go free" (Jn 22:44).

A SPIRITUAL LIBERATION

There are many approaches to human freedom. Philosophers would offer us all possible types of freedom to choose from. "Freedom in general is the state of not being forced or determined by something external, insofar as it is joined to a definite internal faculty of self-determination. Different kinds of freedom are distinguished according to the kinds of pressures which are excluded."[1]

Mortimer J. Adler describes human freedom in these terms:

> *Freedom:* A man who is able (a) under favorable circumstances, to act as he wishes for his own individual good as he sees it
>
> (b) through acquired virtue or wisdom to will or live as he ought in conformity to the moral law or an ideal befitting human nature
>
> or
>
> (c) by a power inherent in human nature, to change his own character creatively by deciding for himself what he shall do or shall become is free in the sense that he has in himself the ability or power whereby he can make what he does his own action and what he achieves his property.[2]

Sociobiologists like Edward Wilson of Harvard would place our human freedom in our ability to perform for the group, the colony, in much the way that insects, birds and animals are free to live for the community. In the freedom of B.P. Skinner, man now controls his own destiny because he knows what must be done and can now know how to do it. But this would rule out any *metanoia* on man's part and deny any gift of freedom from God. E. Marcuse's one-dimensional man puts all liberation within man himself.

Political activists would put all human freedom in liberation from social, political and economic oppression but such liberation theology forgets that unless man is freed spiritually he carries his prison wherever he goes. He substitutes his proletarianism with a new bourgeois spirit which further enslaves him with more enticing bonds of slavery in the material world.

THE SPIRIT FREES

This book deals with the power of the Spirit of Jesus to effect man's total freedom. This is conceived as a gift that is continuously received by man as he seeks to place Jesus Christ, the Logos of God, at the center of his life. The Christian freedom that Jesus came to give us consists in a spiritual revolution of the mind as St. Paul writes:

> Your mind must be renewed by a spiritual revolution so that you can put on the new self that has been created in God's way in the goodness and holiness of the truth (Ep 4:23-24).

Jesus spoke of freedom and His ability to set us free: "If you make My word your home you will be my disciples, you will learn the truth and the truth will make you free" (Jn 8:31-32). Yet rarely beyond these words does He speak formally of freedom. His work during His lifetime was to set us free! He preached the coming of the Kingdom of God and He promised to send us His Spirit who would lead us into all truth.

It is St. Paul who speaks often about the freeing power

of the Spirit of Jesus. The Spirit of Jesus dwells within us, making our bodies temples of God (1 Co 3:16; 1 Co 6:19). He brings us into direct contact with the Risen Jesus who dwells within us with the indwelling Heavenly Father (Jn 14:23). He is a life-giving Spirit making us truly children of God (Rm 8: 15; Ga 4:6). The love of God abounds in our hearts through the Holy Spirit that is given to us (Rm 5:5).

Where the Spirit operates, it is unto true liberty. He frees us from our "carnal" way of judging ourselves and others and the entire world. He frees us from sin and guilt. His love in us drives away all fear. We become progressively more aware each day of our inner dignity as children of God. We begin to live on that deeper, interior level of communing with the indwelling Trinity.

We change our perception of the world around us. We are no longer bound by our desire to control reality, to fashion it according to our own desires. We let go of our defenses. Freedom in the Spirit allows us to walk in the gentleness of children of God who seek at all times to please the Heavenly Father as Jesus, the freest of all human beings, did.

The freedom that we present in this book is the freedom on a spiritual level that allows us through deeper prayer to turn progressively to God living within us as at our center. Such a freedom is the attainment of wholeness, of integration, of actuating by God's creative, loving grace, the potential He has locked within our created personhood to be fully alive human beings. At a time in history when psychology has become the main commentary to tell people who they are, who is abnormal and who is normal, a theological anthropology is needed in which framework alone can we understand true and ultimate human freedom.

Thus many of the insights developed in this book have come from my reading and praying through the writings of the Greek Fathers and the Christian mystics down through the ages. They understood quite well from reflecting on God's Word in Holy Scripture that our dignity consists in being made according to the image and likeness of God Himself (Gn 1:26). Before a conversion we are not aware of our inner dignity. Nor are we aware of the infinite, perfect love that God has always had for us, individually, in His only begotten Son, Jesus Christ. Without a conversion experience, as an ongoing attitude before God, we shall never continue to grow in God's gift of freedom. For such a conversion experience, we need reflective healing that seriously and daily allows us to sit before the healing love of God in His Son Jesus, the Divine Physician, and cry out in our bondage for deliverance.

FREEDOM IN CONTEMPLATION

God's healing love that comes to us in prayer as we let go of our own doing and enter into a deep contemplation of letting God's love be experienced in the Spirit, pours through us and all of our selfish attachments. The Spirit prays the presence of God as indwelling love when we do not know how to pray words any more (Rm 8:26-27). In a way this book is indirectly a book about deeper contemplation. It seeks to show how contemplation is ultimately a growing experience of God's infinite love within us, constituting us into true children of God, new creatures (2 Co 5:17). As we experience this great love, our lives change because the perceptions of ourselves and of God and of the world change. Sadly but truly, we are the way we perceive ourselves.

In contemplation, God's Spirit is free to communicate directly without words or images of our own choosing and to the degree that we have purified our hearts of all self-centeredness. Like Lazarus we are always coming from the darkness of our dead selves into the light of Christ's presence. We discover in adoring that loving presence throughout the day, in the context of each moment and of each event, that freedom is gained by acting as free persons in Christ. As Jesus freely entered into each moment during His earthly life, with maximum freedom, He took His life and gave it back joyfully to His Heavenly Father as gift for gift received. So likewise, the freed Christian lives freely by taking his life into his own hands and determining each thought, word and deed according to what would most please His Heavenly Father.

These pages are not offered as a definitive work on freedom. It is a gathering of personal insights on how the author conceives freedom from studying and praying through Holy Scripture and the early Fathers and the writings of the great mystics of the Church. This work is humbly offered to the reader in the hope that he or she will be helped in the greatest work of one's life: to become free in the Spirit of Jesus so that one can live consciously in the love of God, bringing forth the fruit of that Holy Spirit. We are as free as we live in love, peace, joy, patience . . . the fruit of the Holy Spirit.

If you, reader, will become a bit freer through the reading of this book, the author also will share in that freedom which is always gauged by love and greater humble service to all who seek to be freed!

George A. Maloney, S.J.
August 15: Feast of Our Lady's Assumption, 1977.

The Freedom of God

True freedom can never be understood except in the context of love. "God is love" (1 Jn 4:8). But true love is always a free gift of oneself to another. Theologians and philosophers might ask the question: "Is God free because He loves or is He love because He is free?" One could gather together all possible meanings of freedom and see how they apply to God.

But with these two words: love and freedom, we touch the basic, awesome mystery of the Trinity. Man's puny words about freedom fall blandly upon our understanding, leaving us only with great confusion. It is in profound and silent adoration that we stand before God, searching to look upon His Holy Face. Not man's philosophical terms but Holy Scripture alone can allow us at least to hide in the cleft of the rock as God passes by us (Ex 33:22-23).

In loving adoration the Holy Spirit speaks in the language of love—silence. Yet He does speak! Lovers seem to say to each other: "Be silent that I may hear you." In silent awe before God's majesty we too rise above the relentless pull of time: past, present and future to enter into the unchanging, uncreated energies of God's loving relations within the Trinity and toward mankind. The love of God has been poured into our hearts by the Holy Spirit which has been given us" (Rm 5:5). In that energizing love within our hearts, we are brought back to time before time *"in illo tempore,"* to quote Mircea Eliade [1] in the first appearance of sacred time when man returns to his origin and source of being.

In silence we learn how to love because in silence we receive God's infinite love for us. By letting go of our own concepts and ideas of God and in a searching cry to "see" Him in the way He wishes to reveal Himself to us, we enter into a new knowledge. Balzac describes this loving knowledge attained in silence:

> Love is a simple spring which has left its flower-surrounded bed of pebbles and with stream or river changes its nature and appearance with every wave and finally pours itself out into an immense peace which seems to be full of monotony to imperfectly developed minds but on the shores of which great souls become absorbed in infinite contemplation. [2]

God reveals to us the ineffable mystery of His nature as a unity of three Divine Persons in mutual loving surrender to each other. God is love and only in this context can we begin to gain some understanding into this awesome mystery.

For the humble, poor in spirit and silent in heart, God speaks in the words of the great Byzantine mystic, St. Symeon the New Theologian:

> I know that He who remains immovable descends.
> I know that He who is invisible appears to me.
> I know that He who is separated from all creation
> takes me within Himself and hides me in His arms.

And I am completely outside of the whole world.
But I, so mortal, so insignificant in the world, contemplate
in myself completely the Creator of the world.
And I know that I will not die
because I am inside of life,
and that I have the entire life that completely flows
out from within me.
He is in my heart;
He dwells in Heaven;
both here and there He is seen by me equally dazzling.
But in what way does all of this happen?
How can I exactly comprehend it? [3]

In such contemplation God is seen as love, diffusing
itself everywhere as light to whomever would open his eyes
to accept the loving light of God's gift of Self. Who shall
ever comprehend how the Father is light; as are the Son and
the Holy Spirit? All make up one light yet three different
Persons loving in their unique way. The Father loves the
Son as Source to New Life, as Mind to its exact meaning.
But He loves the Son in His Spirit of Love, in the Spirit of
freedom. "Where the Spirit of the Lord is, there is
freedom" (2 Co 3:18). But the Son in the freedom of the
Spirit returns the Father's love in total surrender.

TRACES OF THE TRINITY

Anthropologists and psychologists have sought to trace
the vestiges of the revealed Christian doctrine of the Trinity
in non-Christian religions. Carl Jung has pointed out that
the Trinitarian structure is one of the privileged structures
of human thought. [4] He holds that the Babylonian triad of
gods: *Anu, Bel* and *Ea,* represent the beginning of theology.
Anu is the Lord of the heavens, Bel, the Lord of the inferior

kingdom and Ea of the underworld.⁵ Such triads of the
Trinity are found also in Taoism, Hinduism and Buddhism,
showing that the mystery of the Trinity plunges roots into
the depths of God and humanity as well.

But it is only in the New Testament that we receive the
fully-rounded doctrine of three related Persons in a unity of
one nature. It is in the revelation of Jesus Christ that we can
not only believe in the Trinitarian love but through His
Holy Spirit we can also experience this loving Trinity
abiding within us.

MAN SHARES IN GOD'S FREEDOM

We understand something of the intrinsic nature of
God as Trinity in a loving community of interacting Persons
only through their actions in the world of nature and the
cosmos. The first relationship of God in love and freedom is
in a relation of Creator to His multiplied creatures. St.
Irenaeus of the second century describes God the Father
and Creator as touching the world of creatures through His
two hands: Jesus Christ and the Holy Spirit:

. . . the Father planning everything well and giving His
commands, the Son carrying these into execution and
performing the work of creating and the Spirit nourishing
and increasing what is made, but man making progress day
by day and ascending towards the perfect, that is, ap-
proximating the uncreated one.⁶

The whole world is charged with God's energizing
power and love. He creates the world as a gift to man who
stands as His *chef d'oeuvre* or masterpiece, made according
to God's very own image and likeness (Gn 1:26). God
entrusts the riches of the created world to man, "to

cultivate and take care of it" (Gn 2:16). But only man shares in God's freedom, the ability to receive His personal love, the gift of Himself as Father and Spouse of man, and also the horrendous power of refusing God's gift in love.

The Book of *Genesis* gives a divine statement, not only of the first man and woman, but also of our own history of rejecting God. "So she took some of its fruit and ate it . . . Then the eyes of both of them were opened and they realized that they were naked" (Gn 3: 6-7).

GOD'S HOLINESS

But God's freedom and love are proved in His pursuing and forgiving mercy. Here we enter into the very heart of God's *holiness*. Because God is holy, He is perfectly good and beautiful and loving. God in His holiness, not needing us, still freely wishes to offer Himself as gift. If God were less holy, and, therefore, less free and loving, He would have given up on us human beings. His pursuit of us might have stopped at the gates of Eden or in the Sinai Desert or at the Cross on Calvary or even in our latest defection as individuals or as a community of His unloving children. Yet He continues freely to love us, wanting to share His life with all of us.

God's power is shown in freely creating us and the whole cosmos. But His greater freedom is seen in His constancy to take His life and give us a share, through love, in His very own nature.

He calls us to receive His holiness and to become free and holy as He is, to open ourselves to His outpouring love and gift of Himself for us and then to become outpoured gift in free love returned to Him and our neighbors. We are called to be saints or holy people, sanctified by God's holiness (Rm 1:7; 1 Co 1:2). God chose us from the beginning to be holy by the sanctifying power of the Holy Spirit (2 Th 2:13). His aim in creating us is that He:

> chose us in Christ to be *holy* and spotless, and to live through love in his presence, determining that we should become his adopted sons through Jesus Christ. . . . (Ep 1: 4-5).

THE HESED COVENANT

The Old Testament describes God's freedom in giving mankind a share in His divine life in terms of a condescending mercy that partakes of very rich and nuanced insights about His freedom and love. *Aheb* is the Hebrew word that expresses God's unconditional love.[7] It reflects nothing of Israel's deserts, but only the wonderful, free choice of this people by a living and loving God, willing to be their Father.

> If Yahweh set his heart on you and chose you, it was not because you outnumbered other peoples: you were the least of all peoples. It was for love of you . . . that Yahweh brought you out with his mighty hand and redeemed you from the house of slavery, from the power of Pharaoh king of Egypt. Know then that Yahweh, your God, is God indeed, the faithful God who is true to his covenant and his graciousness for a thousand generations . . . (Dt 7: 7-10).

This graciousness is underlined by the use of the word *hen.* It stresses the unmerited quality of God's love for man. God is under no obligation to bestow His kindness. He is completely free in His mercy and care, to give these or not to mankind. But it is the richly nuanced word *hesed* that leads us into the freedom of God's love for us. The emphasis in the word *hesed* is the God's persistence and devotion of love.[8] *Hesed* is the act of loving kindness in God's part in choosing Israel, and through His promise to use His might and mercy to support His people a Covenant is made. This is strikingly brought out in the tender words that Yahweh addresses to His Spouse, Israel:

> I will betroth you to myself forever, betroth you with integrity and justice, with tenderness and love; I will betroth you to myself with faithfulness, and you will come to know Yahweh (Ho 2: 19-20).

JESUS—THE NEW HESED COVENANT

How beautiful is the realization among Christians that the *Hesed* Covenant reaches its peak of God's free love for mankind and His infinite, merciful fidelity when His Word becomes incarnate. Jesus Christ is the New Covenant, the full freedom of God in His Spirit of love to give Himself totally to man. He is the New Covenant whose blood poured out, is unto remission of mankind's sins (Mt 26:28). God so loved the world as to give us His only Son to be the way to true salvation (Jn 3:16).

> God's love for us was revealed
> when God sent into the world His only Son·
> so that we could have life through Him;
> this is the love I mean:
> not our love for God,
> but God's love for us when He sent his Son
> to be the sacrifice that takes our sins away (1 Jn 4: 9-10).

Jesus is God's eternal pledge of loving fidelity. In Jesus

God could say that God "can have no greater love than to
lay down his life for his friends. You are my friends" (Jn 15:
13-14). Such *hesed* love of condescending mercy unto the
last drop of blood is translated by St. Paul from the rich
nuances of the Hebrew word into the Greek word *charis.*⁹

> But God loves us with so much love that He was generous
> with His mercy: when we were dead through our sins, He
> brought us to life with Christ—it is through grace that you
> have been saved—and raised us up with Him and gave us a
> place with Him in heaven, in Christ Jesus (Ep 2: 4-6).

Grace, therefore, is not a *thing* as Christians in the
West so often tend to conceive it. Grace is the loving,
energetic relationships which result when the Father in His
Son through His loving Spirit breaks into our human world
in an *eternal now* act of love-unto-death. The remembrance
of God's great protective, loving exploits that the prophets
and the psalmists exhorted their people to recall in order to
open themselves up to God's saving power is now in the
New Testament the *anamnesis* or remembering of Jesus'
gift of Himself to us on the Cross. "Do this as a memorial of
me" (Lk 22:19).

Jesus is always freely dying for us (Ga 2:20). He is the
perfect image of the Heavenly Father (Col 1:15). When we
contemplate Jesus emptied on the Cross of the last drop of
blood and water (Ph 2:10), we see the Father's free love for
us (Jn 14:9; Jn 15:9).

In the new *Hesed* that is Jesus, love cannot remain
uninvolved in the sufferings of God's beloved people. The
Father is in His Word. The Word has meaning only as a
communication, a revelation of the Mind of God.

GOD AMONG US

In the Old Testament Covenant, God revealed Himself as Yahweh who is, but who, in His total *isness,* is always present among His oppressed people, liberating them from all enemies. He is on the side of His enslaved people in Egypt. "And so I have resolved to bring you up out of Egypt where you are oppressed ... Yahweh, the God of the Hebrews, has come to meet us" (Ex 3:17-18).

Yahweh frees His people oppressed not only by foreign powers but also by their own enslavement to selfishness. God speaks in Isaiah of the sign of His freedom to set His people free from themselves, manifested in free love shown for the oppressed around them:

> ... to break unjust fetters
> and undo the thongs of the yoke,
> to let the oppressed go free,
> and break every yoke,
> to share your bread with the hungry,
> and shelter the homeless poor,
> to clothe the man you see to be naked
> and not turn from your own kin?
> Then will your light shine like the dawn
> and your wound be quickly healed over.
> Your integrity will go before you
> and the glory of Yahweh behind you.
> Cry, and Yahweh will answer;
> call, and he will say, 'I am here' (Is 58: 6-9).

God is saying that He is a free God and a freeing God when man accepts His loving presence and thus becomes, like God, free and capable of liberating his neighbor who is in bondage. Now in Jesus is God's loving presence made manifest. This is the sense in which Jesus claims the fulfillment in Himself of Isaiah's prediction when He read the following prophecy in His home-town synagogue:

> The spirit of the Lord has been given to me,
> for He has anointed me.
> He has sent me to bring the good news to the poor,
> to proclaim liberty to captives
> and to the blind new sight,
> to set the downtrodden free,
> to proclaim the Lord's year of favor (Lk 4: 18; Is 61: 1-2).

This is the Good News that Jesus preached. The Kingdom of God was breaking in upon them in His very person. Faith in Jesus, to accept life in Him, came only by the Holy Spirit. "No one can say, 'Jesus is Lord' unless he is under the influence of the Holy Spirit" (1 Co 12:3). The Spirit leads us into the whole truth of the Gospel (Jn 16:13). He convinces us of truth, that Jesus is "the Way, the Truth and the Life" (Jn 14:6). He allows us to remain as branches fed by Christ the vine (Jn 15:1) in order to bring forth great fruit of love toward others.

THE FREEING SPIRIT

We cannot experience God's freeing love except through the Holy Spirit. He gives us the power that He gave to Jesus, the first-born Son of the Father, to say always "Abba, Father" (Rm 8:15; Ga 4:6) and to know we are no longer slaves but freed children. In another chapter we shall develop how the Holy Spirit leads us into the liberty of children of God. Here we wish only to show how the Spirit reveals to our consciousness in prayer the freedom of God who freely loves us in our oppression and sets us free by allowing us to commit ourselves completely to Jesus as Lord.

Thus grace is not primarily a thing, not even an infusion of knowledge about Jesus and the relevance of His Gospel for our Christian living. Grace is Jesus, the Image of the Father, through the loving and freeing Spirit, breaking in upon us at each moment of our daily lives. "Come, follow Me" He calls out to us. In Him we see the *Hesed*-fidelity to us.

> Before the world was made, He chose us, chose us in Christ,
> to be holy and spotless, and to live through love in His presence,
> determining that we should become His adopted sons, through Jesus Christ
> for His own kind purposes,
> to make us praise the glory of His grace,
> His free gift to us in the Beloved,
> in whom, through His blood, we gain our freedom,
> the forgiveness of our sins.
> Such is the richness of the grace
> which He has showered on us
> in all wisdom and insight (Ep 1: 4-8).

The Holy Spirit is the seal that stamps us with the promise, the pledge of our inheritance which brings freedom for those whom God has taken for His own to make His glory praised (Ep 1:13-14). This Spirit of God has made His home in us, St. Paul says (Rm 8:9). Thus our bodies are sacred temples of God because of His Holy Spirit that dwells in us (1 Co 3:16; 1 Co 6:19). We become alive by the Spirit so we must walk always by the Spirit (Ga 5:16). His primary function is to create in us the new life of God in Christ Jesus. Where the Spirit is, there is freedom (2 Co

3:17). The Spirit frees us from slavery "to enjoy the same freedom and glory as the children of God" (Rm 8:21).

REDEMPTION

In the Old Testament the Hebrew word *padah* is used in many human and social relations to indicate some form or other of redeeming of a slave, a process of freeing a person from bondage. Yahweh redeems Israel, the first-born of God among all the nations. When God brought Israel out of Egypt, He was redeeming His son and spouse from bondage. He also was redeeming His first-born son.

Jeremiah reports the words and promise of Yahweh that against all enemies, He will be with His people, "because I am with you to save you and to deliver you from the hands of the wicked and redeem you from the clutches of the violent" (Jr 15:20-21).

But God in His free love for mankind, redeems His people by the *go'el* (Hebrew for an avenger of blood) that is Jesus Christ. Jesus effects the new *Hesed* Covenant by His death on the Cross," . . . and so Jesus too suffered outside the gate to sanctify the people with His own blood" (Heb 13:12-13).

Knowing that Jesus is God's free love, totally given to us on the Cross, we can rejoice in such a Redeemer. He has the power if we accept through His Spirit the inner knowledge for our "hidden self to grow strong, so that Christ may live in your hearts through faith, and then, planted in love and built on love, you will, with all the saints, have strength to grasp the breadth and the length, the height and the depth; until, knowing the love of Christ, which is beyond all knowledge, you are filled with the utter fullness of God" (Ep 3:17-19).

The *good news* that Jesus Redeemer brings is that God has freely pursued us, loved us so that we can partake similarly of God's freedom and His ability to love the whole world. For this reason the Psalmist anticipated the "glory to God in the highest" of the angels who announced this liberation to the little ones, the shepherds in the fields of Bethlehem, when he sang about the Messiah:

> He will free the poor man who calls to Him,
>   and those who need help,
> He will have pity on the poor and feeble,
>   and save the lives of those in need;
> He will redeem their lives from exploitation and outrage,
>   their lives will be precious in His sight. . . .
> Prayer will be offered for Him constantly,
>   blessings invoked on Him all day long. . . .
> Blessed be His name forever,
>   enduring as long as the sun!
> May every race in the world be blessed in Him,
>   and all the nations call Him blessed!
> Blessed be Yahweh, the God of Israel,
>   who alone performs these marvels!
> Blessed forever be His glorious name,
> May the whole world be filled with His glory! (Ps 72: 12-19).

PRAISE FOR LIBERATION

The result of "understanding" by the Holy Spirit the immense love of God freely given to us through Jesus Christ is that we learn freely and spontaneously to praise God and to give Him glory by all we do, think and say. St. Peter describes the vocation of the people of God:

> But you are a chosen race, a royal priesthood, a consecrated nation, a people set apart to sing the praises of God who

called you out of the darkness into His wonderful light. Once you were not a people at all and now you are the People of God; once you were outside the mercy and now you have been given mercy (1 P 2: 9-10).

This is why Christians can rejoice and be glad, praising God in hymns and psalms, by the joyful dance that is their daily life in the Risen Jesus. Jesus, the divine-human Orpheus, has announced a new world, a new creation. "And for anyone who is in Christ, there is a new creation; the old creation has gone, and now the new one is here. It is all God's work. It was God who reconciled us to Himself through Christ and gave us the work of handing on this reconciliation" (2 Co 5:17-18).

We have encountered God's freedom and love in Jesus who by His Spirit allows us to share in that freedom and love as we love the whole world now in Him. We join Jesus as He sings His *Hallel* to the Father. He is the first fruits (1 Co 15:23), the first-born of people made by Him into "a line of kings and priests to serve our God and to rule the world" (Rv 5:10). Why should we Christians not be filled with joyful praise, eager to share this freeing love with the whole world?

It leaves us with a holy wonderment as we enter into the *"mysterium tremendum"* (the awesome mystery, the term of Rudolf Otto10) of God's holiness. Yet there is a joyful exuberance of children unable to refrain from bursting into dance.

St. Benedict wanted his monks to specialize in three things as befitting freed children in the Spirit. They were passionately to seek the Face of God at all times in all circumstances of their lives. They were to serve one another in loving kindness through obedience to the community and they were to be constant and zealous in their praise of the Blessed Trinity.

One of the most "joyful" Saints in the annals of Christianity is St. Seraphim, Russian hermit of Sarov (†1833). His favorite greeting to another person was: "My joy!" Or he would greet a visitor with the joyful, paschal cry of triumph: "Christ is risen!" His explanation of the joy that the Spirit pours into the heart of the freed Christian who has tasted something of the freedom and love of the Holy Trinity can serve as a fitting close to this chapter on the freedom of God:

When the Spirit of God descends to man and overshadows him with the fulness of His outpouring, then the human soul overflows with unspeakable joy, because the Spirit of God turns to joy all that He may touch. This is that joy of which the Lord speaks in His Gospel: A woman when she is in travail has sorrow, because her hour is come; but when she is delivered of the child, she remembers no more the anguish, for the joy that a man is born into the world. In the world you shall be sorrowful; but when I see you, your heart shall rejoice, and your joy no one takes away from you. Yet however comforting may be this joy which you now feel in your heart, it is nothing in comparison with that of which the Lord Himself said by the mouth of His Apostle that this joy neither eye has seen, nor ear heard; neither have entered into the heart of man the good things which God has prepared for them that love Him. The pledge of that joy is given to us now, and, if from this there is sweetness, well-being and merriment in our souls, what shall we say of that joy which has been prepared in heaven for them that weep here on earth? You, too, my son, have had tears enough in your life; see now with what joy the Lord consoles you while yet here![11]

2

Jesus—The Freest of All Men

The way we perceive ourselves and others determines greatly how we behave toward others. What we consider to be the nature of man and his destiny is constantly reflected in our daily choices, our actions, our words. At earlier periods of history there existed rather common imgages of man's nature and destiny. The majority of people guided their lives along the lines of the Graeco-Roman image of man in that culture before Christianity. Chinese followed the Confucian view of man while the Vedic man was standard for the Hindu race.

Christians followed a vision of man that in the later Middle Ages changed to that of the Renaissance and Enlightened man. But today, especially through the arts of communication, TV, radio and the written word, there is no one predominant image of man.[1]

MODERN IMAGES OF MAN

Today, literary authors and philosophers have fashioned for us a *pantheon* of human models for our guidance, but also the mass media with its power of manipulation[2] has created a variety of images of man. Darwin showed that man is "naturally" related to the whole animal world, while Marx showed that man is essentially social by nature. A new society needed to be developed that would end all class societies.

But Arthur Koestler in *Darkness at Noon*3 through his hero, Rubashov, shows us the disaster of sacrificing the individual for an abstract cause. Henri Bergson with his *elan vital*4 and Teilhard de Chardin in *The Phenomenon of Man*5 present us with man in process of *becoming* human in the matrix of a creative dynamism of interacting relationships in love.

Man hides a mystic underneath the struggling, sinful, failing human nature according to T.S. Eliot and Georges Bernanos. Sigmund Freud and Carl Jung give us the psychological man while Erich Fromm shows man as basically pragmatic, seeking to find meaningfulness by living productively.

Reacting against the abstraction of idealism, existential philosophers like Friedrich Nietzsche, Jean-Paul Sartre, Soren Kierkegaard, Paul Tillich, Albert Camus and Martin Buber depict man as struggling for meaning in the existential *Sitz im Leban* in everyday living with its share of absurdity and confusion.

TABLOIDS, NOVELS AND TV

If we are influenced by what we read and see, tabloids, detective novels, TV programs and advertising are fashioning a great variety of images of man that keep flashing kaleidoscopically over his consciousness to attract him to act now in this way, now in that, but self-centeredness and confusion seem to be the key characteristics.

Erle Stanley Gardner has sold more than a hundred million copies of his detective stories, which number has been easily eclipsed by Mickey Spillane. C. LaFarge describes Spillane's heroes as characters basically evil, sadistic and immoral living a life of sadism in which any means is justifiable.[6]

"Playboy" is read each month by three million adolescent males of all ages and immaturity and constitutes a powerful image-creator. Hugh Hefner's philosophy is a man "living life to the hilt," a euphemism for a life of self-centered, pleasure gratification by using women as "things" to be played with in the pursuit of fun.[7]

TV has given us a composite image of bland man, bored with life, seeking by violence to find some way out of his ennui. The gross commercialism has presented man as an insatiable consumer absolutely needing the latest soaps, the newest dog and cat food. Man soon seems more like a manipulated automaton ruled by good old Hal who programs him as to what man should desire and then sends him out to fulfill his desires.

MAN—THE DIVINE ICON

But man sits in the narrowness of his shrunken world, confused, yet somehow suspecting that he was made for something greater. Does not Holy Scripture call him a noble creature, made according to God's own image and likeness (Gn 1:26)? His destiny is to be a participator of God's very own nature (2 P 1:4).

How beautiful and noble man is, is described by the Psalmist:

Ah, what is man that You should spare a thought for him,
the son of man that You should care for Him?
Yet You have made Him little less than a god,

You have crowned Him with glory and splendor,
made Him lord over the work of Your hands,
set all things under his feet (Ps 8:4-6).

His greatness consists in being so loved by God that He
gave to each human being His own Son, the Word enfleshed, " . . . so that everyone who believes in Him may not
be lost but may have eternal life" (Jn 3:16). Under the
illumination of the Spirit of Jesus man is called into an
ongoing experience that he is a son of a loving Father (Rm
8:15; Ga 4:6).

Jesus Christ is the image of the invisible God (Col 1:15)
according to whom man has been created. Man grows into
his human greatness by responding to the call of Jesus to
become one with Him, a loving child of the Heavenly
Father. It calls for a free decision on the part of man to
accept a submission to Jesus Christ, to become the unique
person God has called the individual person to become in
His Son Jesus.

Emil Brunner describes this awesome responsibility
given to man to respond freely to God's call:

The necessity for decision, an obligation which he can never
evade, is the distinguishing feature of man. . . . it is the
being created by God to stand 'over-against' Him, who can
reply to God, and who in this answer alone fulfills—or
destroys—the purpose of God's creation.[8]

THE IMAGES OF JESUS

But to aid us in this awesome responsibility, there is
Jesus, the Image of God. But do we all have the correct
image of God's Image? If we behave according to the image

of man which we perceive as valuable for us, will we not respond to Jesus according to the image we entertain of Him? When we look over the history of Christianity, we see an amazing variety of images of Jesus proposed by Christians and venerated by them to give them the meaningfulness they desired in selecting their images.

Malachi Martin presents us with a scheme of the Jesus figures that developed down through the ages.[9] Besides the non-Christian Jesus figures of Jesus-Jew (from about A.D. 50) and Jesus-Muslim (from about 7th century A.D.), pre-Reformation Christians developed the images of Jesus-Caesar, Jesus-Monk, Jesus-Pantocrator, Jesus-Doctor and Jesus-Torquemada (of the Inquisition).

After the Protestant Reformers (c. 1521), Jesus figures developed for the emotional man from about the nineteenth century. There is Jesus-Jehovah's Witness, Jesus-Christian Scientist, Jesus-Original Gospel Movement, Jesus-Pentacostalist, Jesus-Jesusite and Jesus-Yogi. For the more "reasonable" man there evolved from the eighteenth century types such as Jesus-Apollo, Jesus-Goodfellow, Jesus-Prometheus, Jesus-Anthropopithecus and Jesus-One-of-the-Boys.[10]

Then there is the Jesus to fit the Social Liberationists of the twentieth century of all varieties: the Jesus-Bleeding Lord, the Jesus-Mystic Gun, Jesus-Black, Jesus-Femina, Jesus-Gay, Jesus Christ Superstar and Jesus-Take-My-Marbles-and-Etc.[11]

But the image of Jesus that rings truest to the Gospels and the Jesus encountered by His first followers and the one most moderns desperately search for in their own personal lives is that of Jesus-the free man. Let us look in this chapter at the freedom that Jesus personally enjoyed before we can see the freedom which He came to give us.

THE FREEDOM OF JESUS

The freedom of Jesus cannot be understood except in His relationship to His Heavenly Father. Jesus is perfectly free because at all times He turns inwardly and finds His Father at the center of His being. " . . . I am in the Father and the Father is in me" (Jn 14:11). He is surrounded on all sides and at His center by the surrendering love of His Father in total gift to the Son. Joy, ecstasy, peace and bliss pour over Jesus whenever He turns within and returns the gift of Himself to the Father.

It was in the hours of deep contemplative prayer during the thirty long years at Nazareth and the prayer on the mountain top and in the desert alone with the Father that Jesus learned how to be free. It was in such union as they embraced, surrounded each other, like a mother covering her baby, like two lovers made one in ecstatic embrace, that Jesus experienced the peak of human freedom.

Wrapped in the Father's consuming fire of love, Jesus could only whisper as He would during His public life, "Take all, Father, as You wish. I seek only to please You in all things." He knew in the Father's great love that He was His only Son. In that *eternal now* gaze of the Father, Jesus continually sprang to new levels of awareness that He was sheer gift from the Father.

No separation could hold Jesus away from the Father. He was always "at home" with the Father, "nearest the heart of the Father" (Jn 1:18). The Father is at repose as He has all desires peacefully fulfilled in His Word through the love of His Spirit. Out of such unifying love, Jesus could move into the world of multiplicity, of noise and movement, sin and separation and still be aware of His being God's

Word. He was freed by the Spirit of the Father to walk in the light of the Father's eternal presence and infinite love, not only for Him but for every creature created by the Father.

His mission was to love in that freedom each person He met with the very love of the Father and thus bring the whole created world into a similar freedom. "As the Father has loved me, so I have loved you" (Jn 15:9). The world of darkness lay in separation and alienation. Fears, anxieties, suspicions, doubts, jealousy and hatred divide the children of God. But Jesus, in His prayerful immersion in the Father's loving embrace, was integrated and whole, freed from every estrangement from God and neighbor.

When Jesus preached in the synagogue at Nazareth where, as a boy, He had so often heard God's Word proclaimed, He read Isaiah's text (Is 61:1-2):

The spirit of the Lord has been given to me,
for He has anointed me.
He has sent me to bring the good news to the poor,
to proclaim liberty to captives
and to the blind new sight,
to set the downtrodden free,
to proclaim the Lord's year of favor (Lk 4: 18-19).

His mission was truly to bring each person into the truth that He was the truth, and by accepting Him as the Son of God, man would indeed, like Jesus, be set free (Jn 8:31-34).

FREE TO FULFILL HIS MISSION

Jesus shows on each page of the four Gospels His freedom from doubt about His own inner identity and

therefore His assurance in regard to the goal of His earthly
life. Even though the Father is greater than He and He can
do nothing byHimself (Jn 5:30), yet He knows consciously at
all times that He is one with the Father (Jn 17:21). He
knows clearly His origin and His mission.

> . . . because I have come from heaven,
> not to do my own will,
> but to do the will of the One who sent Me (Jn 7:16).

His word is not His own, but comes from the Father
who is sending Him (Jn 14:24). He is to reveal the Father to
the world. "To have seen me is to have seen the Father" (Jn
14:9). All the attitudes of Jesus towards His fellow beings,
the Disciples, the Scribes and Pharisees, the sick whom He
healed and His listeners who heard Him preach, His words
and actions were all colored by a perfect freedom that was
grounded on his intimate relationship to the Father and His
connected mission. With Jesus, unlike all of us, His mission
was an essential part of His very make-up. He was aware in
His consciousness of being God's Word and He knew that
as Word He had to speak to the human race. " . . . no one
knows the Father except the Son and those to whom the
Son chooses to reveal Him" (Mt 11:29).

He came to preach that the Kingdom of God is close at
hand (Mt 1:14-15), in fact, it was in-breaking in His very
own person. This was to receive life, more abundant life,
that He had come to bring (Jn 10:10). Eternal life was to
know the Father and Jesus Christ, His Son (Jn 17:3).

The "good news" was not only that the Heavenly
Father revealed by Jesus was a loving Father of infinite
mercy, forgiving each person his sins, bringing healing love
to the lonely and desolate, hope to the hopeless, but that the

"in-breaking" of God's energies of love into human lives was being at that moment effected by this man Jesus of Nazareth. This assurance of who He is before the Father, loved infinitely by Him, gives His message a power that knows no hesitation or doubt as to content and direction. He was speaking the truth; He was the very truth (Jn 14:6). His every word, act and conduct was a revelation of God's truthfulness.[1] [2]

FREED FROM PHARISAISM

Rooted in the truth, Jesus was free from any heteronomous spirit that tied Him slavishly to the existing religious doctrines and practices that had become a binding force among the Jews of His time. His Father wanted all men to be freed and Jesus warred against any religious, idolatrous forms and institutions that would prevent human beings from going to the Father.[1] [3]

Jesus was free so as to find the Father working in all things (Jn 5:17). This colored His own conduct toward Jewish law and ordinances and His teaching to others about how they should regard such extrinsic norms. He was faithful in attending services in synagogues and in the Temple in Jerusalem. He healed the lepers and charged them to fulfill the ceremonies required by law (Lk 5:14; 17:14). He paid the Temple tax (Mt 17:27). He came not to destroy the law (Mt 5:17) but to fulfill it (Mt 3:15).

In other matters concerning religious practices enjoined by religious leaders of His time, Jesus could be quite indifferent and even commit violations. He was freed from the abuses concerning the Sabbath rest that a casuistry inflicted as an unreasonable burden on the people. He healed on the Sabbath and showed the Pharisees that the

Sabbath was for God and God would not allow a day to pass if healing were imminently present to the sick in His very presence.

Jesus knew Himself to be the end and goal of the law. He was even what the Temple was all about and once His body was destroyed (Jn 2:19), there would be no need for the material Temple made of stones at Jerusalem. All blood sacrifices were to prepare for His sacrifice of blood unto the › remission of sins (Mt 26:28).

Purification of the outside vessel had no meaning if man's heart was not cleansed by compunction. Fasting and praying were not to be done in an enslavement to custom or to gain the praises of men but were to be done in joy and in hiddenness of one's heart which the Father could see and recompense.

FREE TO BE HUMAN

Jesus could afford to be freely human since all human beings, in God's design, are created according to His image and likeness. No human consciousness ever grew progressively in "unconcealing" the Father's immense, personal love for man as did that of Jesus. At each moment, inside each event, Jesus could "see" His Father working in all things (Jn 5:17). He could "hear" His gracious Father summoning Him into a loving, surrendering obedience and He responded constantly, "Yes, Father!"

Jesus saw the Father present in the warm sunshine that drove away the chill in His bones after a night sleeping outdoors. He praised Him in the simple food and drink that He partook of each day. But especially did Jesus discover His Father freeing Him to be totally human in each human encounter. "In other words, it implies that real humanity exists in him in a supernatural, super-human, divine-human way, that Christ is 'Man' in the way that only God can be: in Mersch's phrase, 'divinely human.' "[14]

Freed from all insecurity before God and man, Jesus spontaneously opened Himself completely to each person, friend or enemy, and loved them with the same love that His Father had for them. All aggressive, nervous moods were dispelled by the gentle love with which Jesus loved each person. His eyes were mirrors that reflected the loving gaze of the Eternal Father. His touch upon the maimed, the demon-possessed, the sinner or a beloved friend brought the healing power of God into all who accepted His love.

Thus at each moment Jesus was freed from anxieties and worries as He opened Himself to cooperate with the loving activity of His Father. He was freed from all impatience at His own human limitations, at the failures and sinfulness of those around Him, including His Disciples. He possessed a marvelous freedom of heart, a spontaneity and completely at-homeness with the human scene.

Yet His openness to be guided by the Spirit of His Father gave Him also an inner self-discipline, even an austerity, in His relationships with all human beings, especially His beloved friends.

His mother, disciples, friends were not His ultimate concern.

He did not merely use them as instruments to glorify the Father but they were diaphanous points of finding the Father in the human context and to return love to Him by serving each human person encountered.[15]

There was that inner sanctuary in His "heart," where He was most Himself; freed of any selfishness, wanting to have only His Father as the perfect center of His life, of all affections and desires. At the converging of His will with that of His Father, Jesus was able to swing free from all that is temporal, finite, of this world, and drown Himself in the *eternal now* of the Father's being. There Jesus grew into freedom. There the Father shared with Him His very own freedom, to love the world and each human being as a point of self-surrender in perfect love.

FREED FROM SIN

A Sufi proverb says:

What the sun is,
Only the sun can teach us.
He who would learn
must towards it turn.

Jesus was so free from sin that not only did His disciples and even His enemies witness to it but He Himself speaks assuredly of Himself as sinless. John the Baptist is given a vision of the Lamb of God, spotless, who is to take away the sins of the world (Jn 1:29-30). Jesus claims there is no injustice in Him (Jn 7:18), that He always does what pleases His Heavenly Father (Jn 8:29), that Satan has no power over Him (Jn 14:30).

Jesus throws out to the Pharisees the daring challenge: "Can one of you convict me of sin?" (Jn 8:46). Only holiness, true freedom from sin at all times and in all circumstances, could claim this. Because He was sinless, He could forgive sins as God could. He also delegates this power that is equally His as it is that of His Father who has given Him power of judgment and His judgment is true (Mt 9:2; Mk 2:3; Lk 5:18; 17:47; 23:43; Jn 5:14; 8:11). His blood, He declares, will be poured out unto the "remission of sins" (Lk 22:20; Mt 26:28 Mk 14:24).

St. Peter declares, "Why, Christ himself, innocent though he was, had died once for sins, died for the guilty, to lead us to God" (1 P 3:18). St. John teaches that Jesus Christ " . . . appeared in order to abolish sin, and that in Him there is no sin" (1 Jn 3:5).

TEMPTED AS WE

In spite of the freedom that Jesus had from sin, He was still tempted. " . . . but we have one who has been tempted in every way that we are, though He is without sin" (Heb 4:15). His human growth consisted in the existential struggle for unity between His consciousness and unconscious. As Jesus learned to live in greater interiority by centering all of His thoughts, words and actions upon the indwelling Father, He learned to let go of the control He exercised over His own human existence. The temptations in the desert and those in the agony of Gethsemane and on the Cross show us something of Jesus entering into the inner combat to win the gift of freedom through a new victory of self-abandonment to His Father.

At the core of the temptations that Jesus underwent was the struggle between a state of independence away from submission to His Father and that of free surrender in loving obedience to the Father's will.

Freedom for Jesus as for us is God's gift but it is won by a great struggle wherein the isolated Self surrenders to the true Self in love, freely given. Without conflict, even in the development of Jesus' human freedom, there could be no growth in freedom.

As Jesus enters into His last and greatest temptation

on the Cross, obedient unto death (Ph 2:8), He reaches a
oneness with the Father never before experienced in His
human consciousness. He reaches also the peak of His
freedom, both in being the true Son of His Father by loving
surrender and also in being the actualized, perfect Image of
the Father's love for mankind. Freedom is taking one's life
in hand to dispose of it so as to be perfectly in conformity
with the mind of the Father. This freedom comes to Jesus
only in the *exodus* experience on the Cross as He passes
over from gift received to gift returned to the Father.

A CONQUERED CONQUEROR

Kahlil Gibran writes beautifully about Jesus:

> There are three miracles of our Brother Jesus not yet
> recorded in the Book: the first that He was a man like you
> and me; the second that He had a sense of humor; and the
> third that He knew He was a conqueror though
> conquered.[16]

Jesus on the Cross, in gifting the Father with Himself
in total surrender, seemingly is conquered by His own
human creatureliness. His love for the Heavenly Father
pours out of His heart, hurling Him into the embrace of
death. He cries out in the pain of not being able to pass over
HIs limitations, "It is finished!" There is no more of self He
can give. Yet that is His cry also of victory. He is the
Conqueror over sin and death. The *Man,* in the first fruit of
the whole human race, has passed over the limitations of
the finite, historical and has brought our humanity into
God's *eternal now.*
St. Paul understood this freedom of passing from the
slavery to self-containment into a freedom that could only

be described as a slavery to Jesus Christ (Co 7:22; Ga 1:10; Rm 1:1). Jesus enters into the Father's freedom by delivering Himself up unto death for love of Him.

Carlyle wrote, "Now and always the completeness of a man's victory over Fear will determine how much of a man he is."[17] We could say in the case of Jesus that He shows us both how much of a God and a Man He is in freely allowing Himself to be conquered by death because only in that act does He become one with the Father, the Conqueror of all death. Out of such darkness and shame Jesus is glorified by His Father.

But God raised him high
and gave him the name
which is above all other names
so that all beings
in the heavens, on earth and in the underworld,
should bend the knee at the name of Jesus
and that every tongue should acclaim
Jesus Christ as Lord,
to the glory of God the Father (Ph 2: 9-11).

The Father glorifies the Son by sending us His Holy Spirit who reveals in Jesus' death that He truly conquers death and all other enemies to God's life, to His Kingdom, the Gift of God Himself to us, His children. St. Paul sings the glories of Christ's victory in which we are to participate:

After that will come the end, when He hands over the kingdom to God the Father, having done away with every sovereignty, authority and power. For He must be king until He has put all His enemies under His feet and the last of the enemies to be destroyed is death, for everything is to be put under His feet though when it is said that everything is subjected this clearly cannot include the One who subjected everything to Him. And when everything is subjected to Him, then the Son Himself will be subject in His turn to the One who subjected all things to Him, so that God may be all in all (1 Co 15: 24-28).

FREEDOM IS HARMONY

The personality of Jesus has been subjected to detailed analysis by psychologically oriented authors. Some find Him to be the Hamlet-melancholic type obsessed by the question: "to die or not to die." Others find Him quite choleric as He, in bursts of anger, cleanses the Temple, screams at Peter and calls the Scribes and Pharisees insulting names.

His calmness in the face of storms and before His crucifiers leads others to brand Him as phlegmatic. Jesus appears still to others as a bit sanguine in His sudden switches from triumphal joy as He enters into Jerusalem on a donkey to weeping (Lk 19:37, 41).

Most of us human beings have our unique personality by an over-emphasis of one or two predominant characteristics and through the insufficiently developed other characteristics. From the Gospel picture of Jesus we see Him as the freest of men precisely because He unites in a harmonious whole all the human characteristics that make up human personality and uniqueness. In every situation He responds with the fullness of His being, with the intense consciousness of knowing His true identity as the Son of the Father. He unites His potential to the loving power of the Father to live each moment according to the good pleasure of His Father.

He moves in freedom before the loving gaze of the Father. The traditions of His race or religion do not control

His attitudes even though Jesus usually respects them and observes them. He loves people, especially the despised and maimed, the prostitutes, publicans, lepers, demon-possessed. He is kind and gentle towards them, pouring the love of the Father into them and healing them.

Yet Jesus also loves to be alone in solitude before His Father. In such moments His living roots plunge ever deeper into the living heart of His Father. He prays alone in the early morning (Mk 1:35). He prays on the mountain top all through the night (Lk 6:12). Yet such moments of deep communion with the Father drive Him back into the world of broken men, women and children. He needs them in order that the burning love for His Father can be released and call Him into a greater awareness that He is the Father's loving Son who at all times seeks to please His Father.

He shows patience to the ignorant and straying sheep, the sinners and cast-off derelicts of society. Yet He manifests also a hardness of character and a forcefulness towards the hypocritical religious leaders. He shows an inner strength of self-possession and a constancy of character; yet He can be tender and completely giving of Himself to a Samaritan woman as though she were the only important person in His life.

Jesus has a universal mission to establish the Kingdom of Heaven. He burns with zeal to bring the good news to all mankind. Yet He can be concerned with practical affairs like feeding hungry people, paying the temple tax, sensitively returning the resuscitated son to the widow of Naim, blessing little children.

In Him body, soul and spirit relationships blend into one harmonious personality of great richness and delicate nuance. Jesus is the freest of all human beings because He constantly lived each moment at the deepest level of His unique "I," that was the perfect Image of God almighty. At that center He consciously felt Himself coming from the Father's free love and in that gift He freely seeks to return Himself as total gift to the Father.

How I love your palace,
    Yahweh Sabaoth!
How my soul yearns and pines
    for Yahweh's courts!
My heart and my flesh sing for joy
    to the living God (Ps 84: 1-2).

Jesus is the human expression, the perfect image of God's freedom which God wishes to share with us. His resurrectional presence to us is to free us from the bondage of all fear, sin and death. There was no freedom under the Law (Ga 3:23) but by faith in the risen Jesus we have been freed from all bondage. "When Christ freed us, he meant us to remain free" (Ga 5:1). Let us now see how Christ, the freest of all men, comes to set us free.

3

JESUS FREES US

God's awesome gift of Himself to us through His Son Jesus in His Spirit comes to us in His gift of freedom. God pursues us in love. He gives us also the frightening power to say *yes* or *no* to His gift. We stand dizzily on the heights of the universe, tempted as Jesus was in the desert, to bow in loving surrender to God's majesty and tender love as our eternal Father or to walk away into the darkness of self-centered love.

One of the most penetrating of modern authors who has grappled with this mystery of human freedom before God's invitation is Feodor Dostoevsky. In his legend of the Grand Inquisitor, told by the "atheist" Ivan to his brother-monk, Alyosha, in the novel, *The Brothers Karamazov,* Dostoevsky tells of the return of Jesus to this earth, this time to Seville of the sixteenth century. After performing a few miracles and arousing the enthusiasm of the crowd for His kingship as the people of old in Palestine did, Jesus is apprehended by order of the ninety-year-old Dominican Cardinal and Grand Inquisitor and is thrown into the dungeon.

The Grand Inquisitor quizzes Jesus, asking Him why He ever came back. The freedom He came on earth to give was too much of a responsibility for human beings to handle. The Inquisitor accuses Jesus:

I tell Thee that man is tormented by no greater anxiety than
to find some one quickly to whom he can hand over that gift
of freedom with which the ill-fated creature is born. But
only one who can appease their conscience can take over
their freedom. In bread there was offered Thee an in-
vincible banner; give bread, and man will worship thee, for
nothing is more certain than bread. But if some one else
gains possession of his conscience—oh! then he will cast
away Thy bread and follow after him who has ensnared his
conscience . . . Instead of taking men's freedom from
them, Thou didst make it greater than ever! Didst Thou
forget that man prefers peace, and even death, to freedom
of choice in the knowledge of good and evil? Nothing is
more seductive for man than his freedom of conscience, but
nothing is a greater cause of suffering . . . Instead of
taking possession of men's freedom, Thou didst increase it,
and burdened the spiritual kingdom of mankind with its
sufferings forever. Thou didst desire man's free love, that
he should follow Thee freely, enticed and taken captive by
Thee. In place of the rigid ancient law, man must hereafter
with free heart decide for himself what is good and what is
evil, having only Thy image before him as his guide. But
didst Thou not know that he would at last reject even Thy
image and Thy truth, if he is weighed down with the fearful
burden of free choice?[1]

It was not freedom that the majority of Christians
wanted from their religion but "miracles, mystery and
authority." Freedom demanded too great a responsibility to
choose according to the image of Jesus and His truth. This
has been the story, not only of sixteenth century Seville but
down throughout the ages to the present day among most
Christians. And yet, Jesus is continually appearing in other
Sevilles, the cities in which we live. In a way He is always

preaching to all who wish to hear what He preached in Nazareth:

> He has sent me to bring the good news to the poor,
> to proclaim liberty to captives
> and to the blind new sight,
> to set the downtrodden free,
> to proclaim the Lord's year of favor (Lk 4:18; Is 61:1-2).

He still whispers into hearts that are open to His coming, "My truth will make you free" (Jn 8:32). We all eagerly seek freedom. But for many of us freedom is our ability to choose from among two or more choices, with no imposition placed upon us from outside agents. We speak of a man who is free in his business, meaning he answers only to himself to work as he wishes. Sexual freedom usually means no restraints. This is applied also to economic and political freedom. Yet enjoying no restraints and no laws would inhibit the freedom of thers. The wealthy in the name of freedom want to continue the *status quo* of exploiting the poor. The poor rebel in the name of freedom wants to share the riches of the wealthy few.[2]

FREEDOM AND THE KINGDOM OF GOD

Jesus rarely spoke about freedom as such. His role was to be the freeing power of God's love come among men. He preached the good news about the in-breaking of the Father's love as synonymous with His very person. He knew one did not reach freedom by hearing a conference about it. People became free by accepting Jesus and His Spirit of love that would make them free in the experience that they now really belonged to God's family, children of God, "heirs of God and coheirs with Christ" (Rm 8:15).

Jesus preached about the Kingdom of God, of the Father's great love for His children. But he came also to actualize this love of God for us by being a perfect image of the Father's love. The good news that made the captives free from their anxieties and fears was not only that God was a loving Father of infinite mercy, forgiving each person his sins, bringing healing love to the lonely and desolate, hope to the hopeless, but that the "in-breaking" of God's energies of love into human lives was being at that moment effected by this man, Jesus of Nazareth. It was not so much the words that He preached that burst the bonds that held the human race in slavery but it was He-Himself, the Word, that was the liberating power if anyone would yield himself to His very person.

If you make my word your home
you will indeed be my disciples,
you will learn the truth
and the truth will make you free (Jn 8:31-32).

But no one could enter into the Kingdom of God unless he turned from his own self-absorption in order to turn completely and freely to God. It was not in new rituals nor in the faithful observance of the Judaic Law that the freedom of Jesus consisted but rather in an inner transformation of the heart. Such a *metanoia* that Jesus preached as the necessary step to true, human freedom was a moving away from the loneliness and isolation, from the state of "unloveliness" into which sin had cast the human race to let God be the complete center of one's life.

But this enlightenment could come only from God's Spirit by way of a new birth. The little ones who, like children, opened themselves to receive God's Word, Jesus Christ, entered into the Kingdom which for Jesus was the same as becoming truly free.

Thus, although Jesus rarely spoke of freedom, still it was to free us that He came. He brought no army to liberate us from the enemy that held us captive. His Father could have given Him "more than twelve legions of angels" (Mt 26:53). But He would use no ruse, no violence or force. He Himself was the sole Liberator pitted against the enemy of darkness that held man's mind in fear.

JESUS IS THE WAY, THE TRUTH AND THE LIFE

Jesus entered into our sinful world, like us in all things save sin (Heb 4:15). He saw human beings enslaved to sin and death and "to the elemental principles of this world" (Ga 4:3). His heart, that was a heart "nearest to the Father's heart" (Jn 1:18), went out to the broken ones who were like sheep without a shepherd (Mt 9:36). When He looked upon the maimed, the blind, the lepers and the paralytics, the epileptics and the possessed, the sinners bound by hatred for others, by lust and pride, He, as it were, could not but be compassionate, full of mercy and loving as His Father is. Faced with the power of darkness and sin and death covering the face of man, Jesus burned with zeal to bring the light of God's love to destroy the effects of sin.

Jesus came to free the whole man, body, soul and spirit, in all of his relationships. He came to give men life that they might have it more abundantly (Jn 10:10). His love, which was an exact image of the love of the Father for His children, poured over each person that He met. He looked into their eyes and poured out an infinite love of healing that, to those who believed and accepted that love, brought them into a new existence.

BY HIS WOUNDS WE ARE HEALED

Jesus came to image the Father's love, not only in each personal encounter with each individual sick person whom He healed when there was faith offered to Jesus, but above all in His final hour of *kenosis*. It was on the Cross that Jesus speaks God's Word of total love for us human beings. Emptied not only of all human dignity but of the very last drops of water and blood, Jesus by that act, has entered into an eternal act of always *now* loving us with such madness. If St. Paul could experience the inner freedom that came from his constant realization that He "loved me and sacrificed Himself for my sake" (Ga 2:20), so we can at every moment experience a freeing from sin and loneliness, fear and anxiety as we reflect upon God's freeing Word.

Our daily life shows us the great need we have for the liberation that Jesus comes to bring us. With a little sincere reflection upon the way we perceive ourselves in relationship to God and to other human beings, we all too often see ourselves in isolation. Our *ego* tells us we are independent; we need no one else. Sin is the thinking and acting out of such a perception. It is a "bias towards self." I must take my life in hand and determine for myself my ultimate direction. My judgments are made in an attempt to keep alive such a belief that I need no one. Ultimately sin is the rejection of love, which is a humble movement toward another to give ourselves to the other instead of holding on fiercely in self-possession of our life.

In such a state we desperately seek to be loved by God and neighbor. Yet our self-absorption resorts to power and attack in order to retain the original perception of our independence from all others. In the words of the lawyer in Albert Camus' *The Fall,*

> Fortunately I arrived! I am the end and the beginning; I announce the law. In short, I am a judge-penitent . . . Ah, *mon ami,* do you know what the solitary creature is like as he wanders in big cities?[3]

Jesus comes as God's great love manifested. He wishes to free us from the isolation into which sin has cast us. With St. Paul we confess that sin in our members has control over us. Wretches that we are, we can be saved only by God's power in Christ Jesus (Rm 7:24). Our strength is in Jesus Christ who alone can save us from our false selves and lead us into the true persons we were meant to be in Him.

> . . . but if anyone should sin,
> we have our advocate with the Father,
> Jesus Christ, who is just;
> He is the sacrifice that takes our sins away,
> and not only ours,
> but the whole world's (1 Jn 2: 1-2).

FREE TO LOVE

Holy Scripture presents man created according to God's own image (Gn 1:26). Man alone, unlike all other created, material beings, stands uniquely as a free agent in communication with God as He freely shares His very life with man. God's gift of Himself was a process of self-giving to man as man worked to fashion a world in loving obedience to his Heavenly Father's wishes. By sin man lost his sonship to the Father Jesus reveals in word and deed God's forgiving love by becoming God's Hesed Covenant of condescending love unto death. His Spirit sent into our hearts gives us an abounding love (Rm 5:5). Jesus and His Spirit bring us into true filial freedom by teaching us the honor and dignity it is on our part to love and obediently serve God.

No longer are we bound to serve our selfish interests, but like Jesus, as St. Paul tells us, we are not to think of ourselves, but think in loving service of our weak neighbors. "Christ did not think of himself" (Rm 15:3).

In the Cross of Christ freedom is revealed as a gift. The Christian under the Spirit of Jesus understands that slavery to egoism is destroyed by Jesus' great personal love for each of us individually. And true freedom is now revealed as God's love in us bringing us into a slavery to belong now totally to Jesus Christ.

How beautifully St. Paul experienced in his conversion that true freedom which was total surrender to Jesus Lord. As Jesus is the "Yes-servant" to His Father, so Paul and other Christians are to pass-over from the slavery to selfishness, sin, death, the law and the elements of this world that kept the entire cosmos held in bondage (Ga 4:3) into a loving service to Jesus Christ.

Paul, after his conversion, saw his freedom in being dead to sin and alive to God in Christ Jesus (Rm 6:10-11). He was "to be in Christ," Paul's favorite phrase that he uses about 164 times to indicate his very real, intimate union with Christ. Christ lives now as the directing force within Paul's life (Ga 2:20). He knew himself to be no longer a slave but a son of God because of the Spirit of Jesus in his heart:

> The proof that you are sons is that God has sent the Spirit of his Son into our hearts: the Spirit that cries, 'Abba,

Father,' and it is this that makes you a son, you are not a
slave any more; and if God has made you son, then He has
made you heir (Ga 4: 6-7).

The good news is that, before Paul's conversion to
Christ, he was a child of wrath by nature (Ep 2:3) but now
through Baptism he has become like Christ, a true son of
God (*huios*) (Rm 8:14, 19; 9:26; 2 Co 6:18; Ga 3:26; 4:7).

With St. Paul, all of us Christians share in Christ's own
life, who now gloriously is risen and lives within us. Yet He
must be further formed within us (Ga 4:19). This new
freedom is one of service, of living, not only as Jesus lived
but living in union with Jesus through the loving power of
the Spirit of Jesus that He constantly releases within our
hearts. By yielding to the life-giving presence of Jesus, we
Christians move from freedom to greater freedom by
gradually being more transformed into the "likeness" of
Jesus. This is the eternal destiny that God had planned for
us before all ages:

> Before the world was made, He chose us, chose us in Christ,
> to be holy and spotless, and to live through love in His
> presence, determining that we should become His adopted
> sons, through Jesus Christ for His own kind purposes, to
> make us praise the glory of His grace, His free gift to us in
> the Beloved, in whom, through His blood, we gain our
> freedom, the forgiveness of our sins (Ep 1: 4-7).

In Christ we are formed into a "new creation" (2 Co
5:17). The old man is now dead and we are alive to Christ
who calls us to service in reconciling the whole world to the
Father (2 Co 5:18-19).

Christ's life within us, that begins as an embryo in
Baptism, is to grow as we cooperate with Christ to live as

free children of God, progressing "to come to unity in our faith and in our knowledge of the Son of God, until we become the perfect Man, fully mature with the fullness of Christ Himself" (Ep 4:13).

GROWTH THROUGH THE HOLY SPIRIT

Christ is to be the center of all our thoughts and actions. Everything in us, the values that we choose to live and act by, must be brought under obedience to Christ Jesus (2 Co 10:5). We are to walk in a new life with Jesus Christ (Rm 6:4). The following chapter will show how the Spirit leads us into full freedom. But here it must be shown how Jesus frees us from everything that is an obstacle to the life of Christ within us through the continued action of the Spirit.

This Spirit has created the new life in Christ within us. He developes it and brings it to its fullness as we yield to the Spirit guiding us. "Where the Spirit of the Lord is, there is freedom" (2 Co 3:17). Thus the truly free life of Christians is guided by a turning within and there to be enlightened in each decision by the movement of the Spirit.

FREEDOM FROM THE LAW

Jesus came not to destroy the Law but to fulfill it. And the essence of the Law was the love of God and the love of neighbor. But when St. Paul speaks of the new freedom that Jesus came to give us through His Spirit he speaks of the freedom from the Law.

Before faith came, we were allowed no freedom by the Law; we were being looked after till faith was revealed. The Law was to be our guardian until the Christ came and we could be justified by faith. Now that that time has come, we are no longer under that guardian, and you are, all of you, sons of God through faith in Christ Jesus. All baptized in Christ, you have all clothed yourselves in Christ, and there are no more distinctions between Jew and Greek, slave and free, male and female, but all of you are one in Christ Jesus. Merely by belonging to Christ you are the posterity of Abraham, the heir he was promised (Ga 3: 23-29).

The purpose of the Law was to hold the Israelites together in a disciplined unity. It was "a beneficent bondage," in the words of George Montague.[4] The child has come of age and now needs no longer the slave-servant to accompany him to school. Faith in Jesus Christ has accomplished the free access to the sonship of the Heavenly Father (Jn 1:12). One has freedom from the Law only to live fully that for which the Law was intended, namely, to love through the power of Jesus' Spirit.

. . . the law of the spirit of life in Christ Jesus has set you free from the law of sin and death. God has done what the Law, because of our unspiritual nature, was unable to do. God dealt with sin by sending His own Son in a body as physical as any sinful body, and in that body God condemned sin (Rm 8: 1-3).

Christians, according to St. Paul, are freed from the Law but not from the obligation that is love. "If you are led by the Spirit, no law can touch you" (Ga 5:18). And the reason is that the Spirit that abounds in our hearts can effect infinitely more than the Law ever could have since the Spirit brings us into the new law of Christ which is to "carry each other's troubles and fulfill the law of Christ" (Ga 6:2). The commandment that Jesus gives us is to love one another as He has loved us (Jn 15:12).[5]

FREED FROM CARES

Jesus came to free us from all the anxieties and fears that come from being over-solicitous in our insecurity to provide security by nervous fretting and worry. This was part of His consistent message that He preached. "But you, you must not set your hearts on things to eat and things to drink; nor must you worry . . . Your Father well knows you need them. No; set your hearts on His kingdom, and these other things will be given you as well. There is no need to be afraid, little flock, for it has pleased your Father to give you the kingdom" (Lk 12:22-32).

According to the teaching of Jesus, the only focus of our striving in our earthly life must be our Heavenly Father. This was how He lived. He sends us His Holy Spirit so that in all events of each momnent we can, in the Spirit, cry out "Abba Father!" (Rm 8:15). Everything: the world, life and death, the present and the future are all our servants, "but you belong to Christ and Christ belongs to God" (1 Co 3:23).

FREEDOM FROM DEATH AND THE POWERS OF THIS WORLD

Jesus frees us from the corruptible, which in St. Paul's vision, is freedom from the absence of God's eternal life living in us. He has come to bring us life and that more abundantly (Jn 10:10). But even this fullness of life is quite compatible with our own physical death in the vision with Jesus who Himself died the physical death in order to enter into an eternal, resurrectional life that He can now share with us. In such faith of the conquering power of the Risen Lord within our lives, we already pass beyond the temporality of living in this material existence or passing through physical death into eternal life. Jesus constantly speaks to us: "I was dead and now I am to live forever and ever, and I hold the keys of death and of the underworld" (Rv 1:18). Therefore, because " . . . Jesus was put to death for our sins and raised to life to justify us" (Rm 4:25), death has no sting, no victory (1 Co 15:55).

Because we have died the greatest death to selfishness and now live unto Christ, we have been truly set free of man's greatest fear of death. It is a fear because it is a threat to our meaningfulness. Man most fears a life of meaninglessness. He has been made by God to live with purpose, to praise, reverence and serve Him. To frustrate this by physical death brings us great fear. It is so crippling a fear that the majority of human beings keep putting off the thought of the end of their earthly life. As Don Juan tells Castaneda:

> You're wrong again. You can do better. There is one simple thing wrong with you—you think you have plenty of time . . . You don't have time.

> My friend, that is the misfortune of human beings. None of us has sufficient time, and your continuity has no meaning in this awesome, mysterious world.[6]

FREEDOM FROM *ME*

This generation has been called the "me generation." I feel certain that all parents in the past, starting with Adam and Eve, must have complained that their children were very *me*-centered. We have to admit, however, that our present age with all the sense pleasures available through

our affluent, technological society is especially prone to
think the whole world exists just for *me!*. No doubt
materialism keeps us absorbed in satisfying ourselves with a
variety of pleasurable experiences and a hurried withdrawal
from anything that means hard work and self-sacrifice into
pain. Lucretius, the Latin poet (96-55 B.C.), insisted even in
his time: "Fear makes gods." Scared and running, the
youth becomes a blustering god with feet of clay. Fear is
written all over their faces as they move into tomorrow,
unsure of anything beyond the beginning of their real
world:- *me!*

Self-absorption has always been a sign of living in a
world of unreal shadows. Jesus promised to free us from
slavery and He insisted that it would mean denying oneself,
taking up the cross and following Him. He alone can break
our idols of ourselves, the slavery of self-obsession, that sin
builds up in us to obtain a sense of false security through
power and attack.[7]

Jesus opens us up to His loving presence. We begin to
live to serve Him, especially and concretely in our suffering
brothers and sisters. We learn to turn the other cheek to
personal hurts and insults, to love our enemies, to go that
other mile. In a word, we become gentle with the gentleness
of Jesus. We put aside our violent aggressiveness and
become a listening presence to see how we can serve others,
how we can live to release their inner beauty by our gentle
going toward them in the love of Jesus' Spirit.

The law of the unredeemed jungle within us is replaced
by the beatitudes of Jesus. Freedom is truly freedom from
our false self to find the true self in relationships of mercy,
gentleness, peace, meekness, poverty of spirit for to such as
are freed by Jesus, the Kingdom of God is given.

FREED FROM ALL FEARS

The list of crippling fears is unending. There is the fear
from human respect, an inferiority complex before more
intelligent people, those wealthier, more beautiful, more
successful than we are. There is disgust from our own
failures and fear of future failures.[8] We may not be free
because our character is too lop-sidedly shy or too in-
dependently over-bearing. Our past habits, sins, thought
patterns, our training and education, our parents and
family life, the list in this direction is so unending of unfreeing factors that we humbly thank God that we are as
normal as we are!

How bound we are with unforgiveness and prejudices
towards others! We are unfree toward the person we just
met for the first time as well as toward our enemies and
even that small group of people who humbly enough call us
their friends.

Then who can describe the fears of the coming day's
events that knot my spirit into a cord with which I beat
myself mercilessly as a tyrant beats a slave into a quivering
submission? How I fear perhaps sickness or that calamity
may strike me today! I may be mugged. I have been lucky
up until now but my turn is coming! Cold fear of each
unknown person I meet possesses me. Fear of car, train or
airplane accident. Fear, fear, fear! God, come to my rescue!

Jesus says:

Come to Me, all you who labor and are overburdened, and I
will give you rest. Shoulder My yoke and learn from Me, for
I am gentle and humble in heart, and you will find rest for
your souls. Yes, My yoke is easy and My burden light (Mt
11· 28-30)

Jesus frees us from all fears by pouring into our hearts the Holy Spirit who dissolves the unreal darkness to bring us into a true knowledge of God's infinite love for us. Knowing who we really are in His love, by faith, hope and love we can embrace each moment and in each event find the freeing love of our Heavenly Father revealed to us in Jesus by His Spirit.[9] The words of St. Paul are discovered to be true: "We know that by turning everything to their good God cooperates with all those who love Him, with all those that He has called according to His purpose" (Rm 8:28).

ROOTED IN HOPE

True Christian freedom is never an end in itself, completely meaningful for the given moment. This moment's freedom to live as completely as we can with God's grace according to our full potential is a freedom that stretches out to sink roots into the far future, ultimately the *eschaton,* the eternal resting in God's unchangeable love.

Freedom is a process of growing into greater freedom as we learn to love all things in God and God in all things.[10] Our freedom, therefore, is built on hope, in God's enduring love in spite of His unapproachableness and beyondness of this given moment. We are here and now free in His love; yet we stretch out to become more free as we allow His love to recreate us into the persons He wants us to be. We hope in His unchanging fidelity even though He seems to be far away from us. We hope in greater glory which means to be freer in our surrender to His love. St. Paul beautifully expresses how true Christian hope frees us:

I think that what we suffer in this life can never ben compared to the glory, as yet unrevealed, which is waiting for us. The whole creation is eagerly waiting for God to reveal His sons. It was not for any fault on the part of creation that it was made unable to attain its purpose, it was made so by God; but creation still retains the hope of being freed, like us, from its slavery to decadence, to enjoy the same freedom and glory as the children of God. From the beginning till now the entire creation, as we know, has been groaning in one great act of giving birth; and not only creation, but all of us who possess the first-fruits of the Spirit, we too groan inwardly as we wait for our bodies to be set free. For we must be content to hope that we shall be saved—our salvation is not in sight; we should not have to be hoping for it if it were—but, as I say, we must hope to be saved since we are not saved yet—it is something we must wait for with patience (Rm 8: 18-25).

A PASCHAL FREEDOM

Through His Resurrection, Jesus Christ is able to touch us in our confirming fears and petty slaveries and lead us out into true freedom. It is His Spirit, who alone can lead us "to know Christ and the power of His resurrection and to share His sufferings by reproducing the pattern of His death. That is the way I can hope to take my place in the resurrection of the dead" (Ph 3:10-12). We are as free as we desire to surrender to the Spirit of Jesus to take away all our fears and even now to live in the freeing power of the Risen Lord. With St. Paul, we can boast of our own weakness (2 Co 11:30) for our total strength is in Jesus Christ. " . . . and by God's doing He has become our wisdom, and our virtue, and our holiness, and our *freedom*" (1 Co 1:30). We are free because "we are those who have the mind of Christ" (1 Co 2:16).

The Risen Lord has conquered in our lives by the

revelation of His Spirit. We are freed from sin and death
and the false values ("the elements of the world") and live
in the freedom of the risen people of God. St. Paul indirectly describes such freedom:

> Here we are, fools for the sake of Christ, while you are the
> learned men in Christ; we have no power, but you are in-
> fluential; you are celebrities, we are nobodies. To this day,
> we go without food and drink and clothes; we are beaten
> and have no homes; we work for our living with our own
> hands. When we are cursed, we answer with a blessing;
> when we are hounded, we put up with it; we are insulted
> and we answer politely. We are treated as the offal of the
> world, still to this day, the scum of the earth (1 Co 4: 10-13).

Jesus is Victor over death and He conquers our hearts
so that we allow Him to be Lord in our lives. Freedom is the
progressive surrender in love to Him so that in each
moment He is Lord. He is the inner force that allows us to
catch this moment of history with all its brokenness, filth,
confining meaninglessness and raise it unto the level of
God's *eternal now.* His Spirit brings us into an ever-growing
awareness of our true dignity before the world. In that
dignity of being loved infinitely by God in Christ Jesus, we
are free to love as He loves us. Freedom, as God gives us this
great gift, is nothing less than the gift of loving ourselves
and the entire world as God loves us and with God's love in
us.

Kahlil Gibran gives us a fitting closing to this chapter
on the freeing power of Jesus.

> The Nazarene was not weak! He was strong and is strong!
> But the people refuse to heed the true meaning of strength.

Jesus never lived a life of fear, nor did He die suffering or complaining . . . He lived as a leader; He was crucified as a crusader; He died with a heroism that frightened His killers and tormentors.

Jesus was not a bird with broken wings; He was a raging tempest who broke all crooked wings. He feared not His persecutors nor His enemies. He suffered not before His killers. Free and brave and daring He was. He defied all despots and oppressors. He saw the contagious pustules and amputated them. . . . He muted Evil and He crushed Falsehood and He choked Treachery.

Jesus came not from the heart of the circle of Light to destroy the homes and build upon their ruins the convents and monasteries. . . . He came to demolish the majestic palaces, constructed upon the graves of the weak, and crush the idols, erected upon the bodies of the poor. Jesus was not sent here to teach the people to build magnificent churches and temples amidst the cold wretched huts and dismal hovels . . . He came to make the human heart a temple, and the soul an altar, and the mind a priest.

These were the missions of Jesus the Nazarene, and these are teachings for which He was crucified. And if Humanity were wise, she would stand today and sing in strength the song of conquest and the hymn of triumph.[11]

4

Where the Spirit is, There is Liberty

Have you found yourself returning to the fables that you read as a child, those famous Grimm fairy tales, and finding new meaning that escaped you as a child? My interest in dreams and a "gentleman's" knowledge of the psychology of Carl G. Jung have opened up for me new levels of application.

I think of that beautiful story of Rapunzel, locked up in a tower and constantly berated by the cruel witch. She was not allowed a mirror or shiny pot to see that she really was a beautiful girl. But the witch convinced her that she was extremely ugly. But one day a prince charming climbed the tower and their eyes met at the window. As Rapunzel looked into his clear eyes, she saw all of her beauty reflected in his love for her. From that moment the witch's spell was broken as Rapunzel knew her true beauty in the eyes of one who loved her.

The majority of us are not free, but we are held captive by the ugly witch of our dark side, our false *ego.* We live in a constant fear of life and of death. By refusing to live at the center of our spirit—to God's Spirit level, we are barraged constantly by fearful thoughts of our unworthiness, of sin and death. We are not integrated, whole people. We are convinced that we are *ugly* and that no one loves us!

Nicholas Berdyaev, the twentieth century Russian philosopher, describes true freedom as a victory in the area of the spiritual world:

Victory not only over the fear of death but over death itself, is the realization of personality. The realization of personality is impossible in the finite, it presupposes the infinite, not quantitative infinity but qualitative, i.e. eternity. The individual person dies, since he is born in the generic process, but personality does not die, since it is not born in the generic process. Victory over the fear of death is the victory of spiritual personality over the biological individual. But this does not mean the separation of the immortal spiritual principle from the mortal human principle, but the transfiguration of the whole man. . . . Freedom must be loving and love must be free. It is only the gathering together of freedom, truth and love which realizes personality, free and creative personality. Man passes from slavery to freedom, from a state of disintegration to a condition of completeness, from impersonality to personality, from passivity to creativeness, that is to say, he passes over to spirituality. [1]

True freedom, therefore, consists in man integrating all levels of his being under the dynamic action of God's love, that in Scripture is called the Spirit of God.

SPIRIT IN MAN

St. Paul describes man's integration as the bringing of *spirit, soul* and *body* into perfection or holiness:

May the God of peace make you perfect and holy; and may you all be kept safe and blameless, spirit, soul and body, for the coming of our Lord Jesus Christ (1 Th 5:23).

We can easily understand, even in the language of the simplest people, that we are made up of body and soul. To understand the concept of man's *spirit* where true freedom takes place, we must go to Holy Scripture. We will see that man's spirit cannot be considered as a static part of man. Man's spirit, in Scripture, will be seen as man viewed in his unique personality through a knowing relationship in love to God.

Neshamah in Hebrew means breath and describes life as found both in God and man.[2] "Then he breathed into his nostrils a breath of life, and thus man became a living being" (Gn 2:7).

The Hebrew word, *ruah,* however, is the usual term in the Old Testament for wind or spirit to indicate God's presence among men and in His creation. It often connotes a presence of God by *power.* If God's spirit is operating throughout all of nature, fashioning both man and all other creatures in a mysterious, awesome way, His spirit is more powerfully operating in His condescending, *hesed* covenantal love for His people. God's spirit comes upon individuals and His entire people to restore them to new love relationships with Him. God is most spirit when He is renewing His people by giving them "a new heart." God breathes His love. Repentance allows His people to open up to receive His breathing-in-spirit of love to become quickened again, to share life-giving relationships with Yahweh.

I shall give you a new heart, and put a new spirit in you; I shall remove the heart of stone from your bodies and give you a heart of flesh instead. I shall put My spirit in you, and make you keep My laws and sincerely respect My observances. You will live in the land which I gave your ancestors. You shall be My people and I will be your God (Ez 36: 26-28).

God's *ruah* will enter into His people and raise them up to a new life in His spirit. The prophet Ezekiel shows us God breathing His breath upon dry bones. "I am now going to make the breath enter you, and you will live; and you will learn that I am Yahweh" (Ez 37:6-7).

God's spirit, in Isaiah's prophecy, is to come upon the Servant of the Lord. "I have endowed him with My spirit that he may bring true justice to the nations" (Is 42:1). The same Servant confesses: "The spirit of the Lord Yahweh has been given to me, for Yahweh has anointed me" (Is 61:1).

THE SPIRIT OF JESUS

In the New Testament the Spirit of God relates to Jesus in two distinct ways. In the most common manner in the Synoptic Gospels, the Spirit has priority, comes upon Jesus and anoints Him. Jesus is first conceived by the power of God's Spirit, is baptized and anointed for His mission by the Spirit. He is driven into the desert by the Spirit. He casts out demons by the Spirit's power, heals and performs all sorts of miracles in the power of the Spirit.[3] God had anointed him with the Holy Spirit and with power (Ac 10:38).

In the Pauline and Johannine writings we find the second manner of the Spirit relating to Jesus. Not only does Jesus receive the Spirit, but He sends the Holy Spirit upon His followers. The Spirit is the Spirit of Christ or of the Son (Rm 8:9; 2 Co 3:17; Ga 4:6; Ph 1:19). Jesus promises that "I will send Him (the Advocate) to you" (Jn 16:7). This is the fulfillment of the meaning of God's Spirit in Holy Scripture. Jesus could not give the Spirit until He had died, St. John observes (Jn 7:39). He had first to receive God's

Spirit before He could share God's Spirit with others. He who was the image of the Father first had to receive in His human life the immense love of God. Then He, dying by the power of so great a love for us, could release that same love within our hearts.

In order to understand more clearly the *freeing* power of the Holy Spirit, let us see that God's Spirit is more than an instrument that Jesus sends into our lives to perfect His people. With this aspect we are all familiar. Without a doubt it is rooted in Scripture. Jesus sends us the Spirit to complete His work on earth (Jn 14:26). The Holy Spirit brings us into the filiation of children of God (Rm 8:15; Ga 4:6).

The Holy Spirit is a creative force that is new and distinct from Jesus. He is a special power different from the power of Jesus. Yet He is tied to Jesus Christ. "We know that He lives in us by the Spirit that He has given us" (1 Jn 3:24). Traditionally we tend to look upon the Spirit as the one who opens us up to Jesus Christ and His redeeming power on the cross.[4] But the New Testament presents the Holy Spirit in a different way. Jesus died, but now He lives!

The Holy Spirit is presented as the new way of existence and action by the Risen Jesus."[5] Jesus is the new Adam. He is the first fruits, the first-born of many sons. Risen, Jesus is what the whole world is to become. The Spirit's work is to be Christ's life-giving Spirit to the world. He draws us into Christ, into His Body. He divinizes us, making us "new creatures" in Christ Jesus 2 Co 5:17).

A LIFE-GIVING SPIRIT

God's exalting Jesus through the resurrection is God's acceptance of the sacrifice whereby Christ, the perfect man, passes over from the condition of flesh (*sarx*), which was subject to death, into the new condition of spirit (*pneuma*) and now becomes the life-giving Spirit, the Head of the new humanity, established by Him as the new people of God through His Spirit. In Christ's death, God condemned sin in the flesh (Rm 8:3). The power of sin and death was broken. The resurrection of Christ is uniquely important because His new and glorious life makes Him the New Adam and the Lord of the Universe, capable now in this exalted existence in glory of bestowing upon us the same life of the Spirit by making us sons of His Heavenly Father.

Jesus insisted that it was imperative that He leave His disciples because if He did not go, the Advocate would not come to them (Jn 16:7). When His human body is glorified by the Father's Spirit, it becomes for all of us the source of the Spirit, of eternal life. Now Jesus Risen cannot be separated from His Spirit. The Spirit is God's life-giving "Breath" that the Risen Jesus is always breathing upon us. We can see why St. John tells us that Jesus could not have given His Spirit before He had died (Jn 7:39).

BODY, SOUL, SPIRIT

We cannot understand our deep, inner slavery or our ultimate dignity to which God has called us as free children of the Heavenly Father unless we see our destiny from all eternity as being by Jesus' Spirit *in Christ*.

The early Greek Fathers built a theological anthropology around the Biblical model of image and likeness. Simply put, from the teachings of the first great Christian theologian, St. Irenaeus of the second century, man has been made by God "according to the image of God," that is, Jesus Christ. Man is not the image of God, but is made in a dynamic relationship of moving the basic "imageness" relationship to that of "likeness."[6] Man, before he is baptized, possesses body and soul relations. God's "breath" in him as a bodied being (*soma* in Greek) allows man to relate as a whole being, a psycho-physical unity, a personality *ad extra*, in relation to the created, material world around him. As body-man, he also has soul relations, the psyche with all the emotions and passions along with the intellectual and volitional life that allows man to relate to other souled-beings.

But *spirit* is not yet in man, born into sin and death of God's deeper life in him. He does not possess, in Irenaeus' words, the *likeness* to Jesus Christ: the conscious, life-in-Christ that only the Spirit of the Risen Lord can bring to man. Man comes into spirit-relationships through a knowing relationship in love to God. Man is *this* individual person because God calls him by his personal name. More so, man is loved infinitely, is really the Son of God because of the spirit-to-Spirit relationships he experiences that he is one with Jesus Risen. He participates in the life of Christ that now conquers all fear, death and sin in his life. He enters into true *immortality* which is more than not dying bodily. Immortality and incorruptibility are synonyms for man's entering into his real personality, as a child of God, a "co-heir" with Jesus Christ of Heaven forever (Ga 4:6).

Let us quote from St. Irenaeus:

Now the soul and the spirit are certainly a part of the man but certainly not the man; for the perfect man consists in the comingling and the union of the soul receiving the spirit of the Father and the admixture of that fleshly nature, which was molded after the image of God . . .

But when the spirit here blended with the soul is united to God's handiwork, the man is rendered spiritual and

perfect because of the outpouring of the Spirit, and this is
he who was made in the image and likeness of God. But if
the Spirit be wanting to the soul, he who is such is indeed of
an animal nature, and being left carnal, shall be an imperfect being, possessing indeed the image of God in his
formation, but not receiving the likeness through the Spirit
and thus in this being imperfect . . . For this reason he
(Paul) declares that those are 'the perfect' who present unto
the Lord the three component parts without offense. Those
then are the perfect who have had the Spirit of God
remaining in them, and have preserved their souls and
bodies blameless, holding fast the faith of God, that is, that
faith which is directed towards God and maintaining
righteous dealings with respect to their neighbors.[7]

From a Biblical, theological point of view, man is
incomplete and imperfect until he enters into an integration
of body-soul-spirit relations with himself, the material
world around him, loving union with other human beings
and ultimately with God. Now we can see that the Spirit of
Jesus is God's breathing into us of His very own loving
energies, drawing us ever more through the events of each
day, the historical perspective, into a deeper, ontological
relationship with the Risen Lord Jesus.

This was the plan that God had for us from all eternity:

Before the world was made, He chose us, chose us in Christ,
to be holy and spotless, and to live through love in His
presence,
determining that we should become His adopted sons,
through Jesus Christ
for His own kind purposes,
to make us praise the glory of His grace,
His free gift to us in the Beloved,

in whom, through His blood, we gain our freedom, the
forgiveness of our sins.
Such is the richness of the grace
which He has showered on us
in all wisdom and insight (Ep 1: 4-8).

THE SPIRIT REGENERATES

We have already pointed out in earlier chapters that
through the Cross Jesus Christ has destroyed eschatological
death and sin. By His own resurrectional life He brings to
us this "new life." "When He died, He died, once for all, to
sin, so His life now is life with God; and in that way, you too
must consider yourselves to be dead to sin but alive for God
in Christ Jesus" (Rm 6:10-11). We are brought into a new
creation through our Baptism.

But when the kindness and love of God our savior for
mankind were revealed, it was not because He was concerned with any righteous actions we might have done
ourselves; it was for no reason except His own compassion
that He saved us, by means of the cleansing water of rebirth
and by renewing us with the Holy Spirit which He has so
generously poured over us through Jesus Christ our savior.
He did this so that we should be justified by His grace, to
become heirs looking forward to inheriting eternal life (Tt
3: 4-7).

Baptism puts us into direct contact with the
resurrected, glorified Christ through the life-giving Spirit.
The Spirit of Jesus Risen dwells within us, making our
bodies temples of God (1 Co 3:16; 1 Co 6:19). He brings us
into direct contact with the spiritualized Body-Person of
Jesus Risen who dwells also within us along with the in-

dwelling Heavenly Father that Jesus promised would come with Him to dwell within us as in a mansion (Jn 14:23).

This is the New Adam, the new creation, the whole Body of Christ. I and you, each individual baptized in Christ, now live according to the new inner principle of life which Christ is, not separated from His life-giving Spirit. St. Paul can say as almost identical the statement that Jesus Christ lives in him (Ga 2:20) and the Spirit of Jesus living within the Christian makes him an adopted child of God (Ga 4:5; 3:26).

True regeneration brought about by the Holy Spirit is a freeing process, a true liberation. No longer is the Christian bound by darkness and illusion. He is enlightened by the light of God's indwelling presence to know the truth, that He is in Christ, a part of His Risen Body, the glorified Jesus. He has been begotten by God as His child (Jn 1:13; Jn 3: 3, 5, 7). The love of God abounds in his heart through the Holy Spirit that is given to him (Rm 5:5).

St. John, the Beloved Disciple, cannot quite get over the Good News as he writes:

Think of love that the Father has lavished on us,
by letting us be called God's children;
and that is what we are . . .
My dear people, we are already the children of God
but what we are to be in the future has not yet been revealed;
all we know is, that when it is revealed
we shall be like Him
because we shall see Him as He really is . . .
No one who has been begotten by God sins;
because God's seed remains inside Him,
He cannot sin when He has been begotten by God (1 Jn 3: 1-2, 9).

PRINCIPLE OF INNER DIGNITY

The freeing power of the Holy Spirit, therefore, consists primarily in an ongoing process of leading us out of slavery from sin and death and the Law into true liberty as children of God. As He reveals to us daily the resurrectional power of Jesus' presence within us, allowing us to live each moment in Him and with Him, we learn to accept our true identity. Living in the present *now*, we can live in the unchangeable eternal *now* of God's love for us in Christ Jesus. This is not a mere static, Platonic *Idea* that we reach by an illumination to discover what was always true—God's perfect love for us from all eternity.

The Holy Spirit progressively effects our regeneration into children of God as we yield to His power in us. The Spirit has liberated us from the slavery of sin (Rm 6:17). We have truly been reborn from above, not merely by water but by the Holy Spirit (Jn 3:5). Yet with St. Paul we can confess that we are prisoners "of that law of sin which lives inside my body" (Rm 7:23).

Yet the Good News is that my rebirth is always taking place at this moment that the Spirit pushes me to live according to my inner dignity of being in Christ, a part of His Body, a child of God.

LIFE IN THE SPIRIT

St. Paul uses the phrase, "in the Spirit," 19 times. But more specifically, we find him using the more specialized term of Spirit to apply to the divine Power, the Holy Spirit, sent by God through the merits of Christ and His intercession to effect the work of sanctification or *christification* of man. Paul assigns to the Holy Spirit the character, initiative and salvific action proper to a person. Through personal experience "in the Spirit," he had discovered the world of the Spirit. It was a "new sphere of life" (Rm 6:4). The work of the Spirit was to create this new life of Christ in the Christian. As we had become alive by the Spirit, so, St. Paul exhorts us, then we must walk by the Spirit (Ga 5:16, 26). Christians are *pneumatikoi,* spiritualized by the Spirit, since the primary function of the Spirit is to create this life in Christ. He sees the world tied together in a hope of being set free from its slavery to decadence "to enjoy the same freedom and glory as the children of God" (Rm 8:20-21). We do not possess the fullness of the spirit but we have come into the "first-fruits of the Spirit" (Rm 8:23). Still we have the pledge and guarantee of its completion (2 Co 1:22; Ep 1:14). Thus we can see that for St. Paul the phrases "in the Spirit" and "in Christ" complement one another.

The Spirit is given in embryonic form in Baptism to bring about the fullness of Christ's life in us by making us conform gradually through progressive growth to a greater likeness to the image of Christ. This life in the Spirit will have an eschatological fruition in the life to come:

> Your interests, however, are not in the unspiritual, but in the spiritual, since the Spirit of God has made His home in you. In fact, unless you possessed the Spirit of Christ you would not belong to Him. Though your body may be dead it is because of sin, but if Christ is in you then your spirit is life itself because you have been justified; and if the Spirit of Him who raised Jesus from the dead is living in you, then He who raised Jesus from the dead will give life to your own mortal bodies through His Spirit living in you (Rm 8: 9-11).

We Christians are caught between two forces: the power of evil and the Spirit of Christ, between the unspiritual in us and the spiritual. We are to live according to the Spirit, the new principle of Christ-like operations within us. The Spirit has created this new life in Christ living within us. He fosters it, stimulates its growth, purifies us from any obstacle to its maturity. He brings this life to its fullness in the proportion that we allow this Spirit to be the normative influence guiding us in our moral choices that determine our true growth in Christ.

Ideally, the life of a Christian should be a "spiritual" one, a turning within, to be guided by the Spirit. No longer is there an extrinsic code of morality, a Judaic Law or any other law operating. Idols constructed by men come crashing down as the Christian gives the Spirit full freedom to work within his human context.

> . . . if you are guided by the Spirit, you will be in no danger of yielding to self-indulgence, since self-indulgence is the opposite of the Spirit, the Spirit is totally against such a thing . . . If you are led by the Spirit, no law can touch you. . . . What the Spirit brings is very different: love, joy, peace, patience, kindness, goodness, trustfulness, gentleness and self-control. There can be no law against things like that, of course. You cannot belong to Christ Jesus unless you crucify all self-indulgent passions and desires. Since the Spirit is our life, let us be directed by the Spirit (Ga 5: 16-25).

HETERONOMY

Nicholas Berdyaev and Paul Tillich have both articulated for modern readers the contrasting forms of spirituality or religious cultures that they call *heteronomy, autonomy* and *theonomy.*[8] It is difficult to know who influenced whom, but Tillich's presentation is the more complete and penetrating.

Nomos is the Greek word for *law*. *Heteros* defines a religious attitude that places authority outside of the interiorized, spiritual powers of the individual, informed by the Holy Spirit and relying upon an extrinsic force to constitute the ultimate authority and guarantor of human development. This can be the religious level of a child incapable for the time being of a higher transcendence than the authority of parents, teachers, priests or ministers. For adults, who do not move into a deeper spiritual development, the extrinsic authority may be some religious leaders, the Bible or other religious writings given a sacredness through tradition or some external rituals.

The intrinsic evil when religion becomes heteronomous is that man is shackled into a slavery to some extrinsic force taking away from him the necessity to evolve further in an opening to the Spirit. Tillich bluntly defines it as demonic. "For the demonic is something finite, something limited, which puts on infinite, unlimited dignity."[9]

John Haughey calls such a spirituality the *programmatic*. He describes such an approach to God as one in which "the person's experience of God has come about in and through the Church. . . . His responses to God, whether liturgical, devotional, moral, or doctrinal, have been framed for him by the teaching, visible Church."[10]

We have all met "religious" persons who "hide" behind the demanding authority of a teaching body of bishops, the Bible in a fundamentalistic interpretation, kosher food practices, Koran injunctions, extreme devotions of a magical type to saints, relics or certain ritual practices. Not all of these are evil or "demonic," to quote from Tillich. But they can never be ultimates in themselves. They must be inserted into a higher level of self-direction. The Holy Spirit frees us from any idolatry of forms and allows us to put all such structures of extrinsic authority into a synthesis permeated by His guidance.

AUTONOMY

As a child grows into adolescence and breaks away from extrinsic authority in order to find himself as an individual with self-determination and an exercise in autonomy of free choice of values, so adults on a religious level and even whole churches or religious groups can move from a heteronomous to an autonomous level. Tillich defines autonomous culture as "the attempt to create the forms of personal and social life without any reference to something ultimate and unconditional, following only the demands of theoretical and practical rationality."[11]

Here man is the center, determining his values without any outside authority and without any other transcendence except his own interiority as he sees things in reference to himself as ultimate. Basically this is a reaction against the former type of religion or spirituality, but it, too, loses any ultimacy or reference in a fresh movement in faith, hope and love to surrender oneself to the interacting of God's love and grace in man's life.

We have all met "religious" persons who are of the reformed type. They are very auto-critical, this-world oriented, seemingly low in a childlike faith. Such a person does not place much importance on rituals or communal services, pious practices or on personal prayer other than time to be quiet to reflect by his own powers where his life is going and what he must do in given circumstances to be a better human being.

The Holy Spirit comes into our lives to free us from a slavery to our own intellectual and volitional powers. He

opens us up to His inner directing power that comes
through prayerful communication. This is the theonomous
level where God becomes the sole, directing law.

THEONOMY

Theonomy is a spirituality in which we place ourselves
under the interior presence of the Spirit operating, as
Tillich calls it, as the divine ground of our being that lies at
the depth of reason. Such a religious approach is able to
inform the heteronomous forms and those of the
autonomous with true meaning since theonomy is rooted in
the ultimacy of God Himself, directly and immediately.

It is rooted in the spiritual presence of God as holy,
both within ourselves and within every atom of the universe.
One is in touch with the "uncreated energies" of God's
loving activity throughout the whole cosmos, but especially
within the lives of individuals. It is the meeting of our *spirit*
and God's Spirit in loving communication. It is rooted in
faith, hope and love whereby we can be in touch with God
in the most personalistic way in each moment of time. It is a
"meta-rational" way of coming to "see" God and to "hear"
him. It is a loving surrender of ourselves into His loving care
as we strive with full power to be in accord with the God-
given potential within us. It is the fulfillment of the
imageness and likeness of God within us. It is an ongoing
process of contemplating the "in-breaking" of God into the
historical that is built up on man's *praxis,* the disciplining
himself from any self-centeredness, that tends always to fall
back to a heteronomous or autonomous level of operating.

The Greek Fathers built a whole mysticism around
what they called *theoria physica* or a *Logos* mysticism. This
was an infusion in an ongoing process by which God fills

the Christian man of prayer who has purified himself of all
idols with an immediate intuition of the *logoi* or the *raison
d'etre* of all things in the *Logos,* the creative power of God
in whom all things are made and in whom all things find
their fullness through the Word's Spirit.[12]

This penetrating into the "insideness" of things,
Tillich is fond of calling the "depth-dimension." This is the
freeing power of the Spirit that allows theonomy to keep
religion from becoming an idol and yet allows the
heteronomous and autonomous elements to reach their full
and proper meaning. Tillich defines this dimension: "It
means that the religious aspect points to that which is
ultimate, infinite, unconditioned in man's spiritual life."[13]

A DIAPHANY OF GOD

For such Spirit-filled Christians the dichotomy between the secular and the sacred, the holy and the profane
breaks down. The Holy Spirit allows such to move through
the various levels of Holy Scripture to penetrate the Spirit's
meaning. Such a person listens to the Spirit speak in each
relationship. He experiences the freeing power of God's
loving Spirit as he puts aside his aggressive moods and
attacking attitudes and gently yields to the movement of the
Spirit in love. He drinks deeply of God's inner beauty in
each flower, stone, the beauties of the seasons, the smile of
a baby, the etched strength in the face of an old man. He
seems to find a meaning beyond rational meaning in the
sufferings, the crimes, the wars and evils perpetrated
against the defenseless. In the words of Teilhard de
Chardin, he begins to see "Jesus Christ shining
diaphanously through the whole world."

God is no longer an object to him. The Holy Spirit has

affected and continues to effect an ever increasing inner communication and interpenetration. Such a Christian enters into God who is no longer far away, but St. Paul's wᵣ ds become an experience: "Yet in fact He is not far from any of us, since it is in Him, that we live, and move, and exist . . . " (Ac 17:28). The sacraments, especially that of Holy Eucharist, become living realities that continue the presence and transforming power of the Holy Spirit. The Eucharist is lived, as St. Maximus the Confessor calls it, as a cosmic Liturgy. Each breaking of the bread with friend or stranger becomes for such a Spirit-filled Christian a continued living of the Eucharist, the recognition of Jesus in that breaking.

CHRISTIAN MORALITY

Man is to listen attentively under the guidance of the Holy Spirit to the living Word within him. The Spirit reveals to us God's will through the fabric of our daily life, our family, our larger community, the Church, the whole human race. In particular it means to respond to the living Word within us through the illumination of the Holy Spirit through the norm for right conduct which can never be merely an extrinsic law or our own rational way of guiding our conduct. This becomes a response to the living Word in us, a response to the Holy Spirit speaking also within the Church through Tradition and the teaching body empowered by the same Spirit of Jesus to teach us without error. And finally, it is a response to the union with others experienced in the Eucharist which becomes the module experience of our larger union with all human beings.

Jesus Christ did not give us a highly involved moral system. St. Paul and the other New Testament writers also did not want to present us with another Law. We are under a new law: " . . . the law of the Spirit of life in Christ Jesus has set you free from the law of sin and death" (Rm 8:2). Charity or *agape* is the touchstone to the law of the Spirit. It was divine love that moved God to send us His Son. That same love is powerful enough in us to uproot inordinate self-love which holds us in slavery.

LOVE OF NEIGHBOR

True freedom is self-determination in the inmost depths of being. It is opposed, as has been pointed out in previous chapters, to every kind of external determination which is a force or compulsion from without or from within. We enter into true self-determination only when, in the depths of our meaning, we touch God's Spirit who releases our spirit to become a loving movement in freedom toward others. True self-determination and self-giving love to others become synonymous and are the freeing work of the Holy Spirit. The fruit of the Spirit is love . . . (Ga 5:22).

And the basis for true love for other human beings is always the love of God that is experienced within our inner spirits. This is not only the work of the Holy Spirit. This ultimately is what the Holy Spirit is. He is the applied love of the crucified Jesus, now risen and living within us by the indwelling Spirit. Jesus is one with the Heavenly Father, living within us and loving us in that eternal, unchanging love. In prayer, the Spirit comes to our spirit and bears united witness that we are truly loved as the Father loves His eternal Son (Rm 8:15). God's very own dynamic current of love, between Father and Son, catches us up and regenerates us into new creatures, ever-more consciously aware of our inner dignity of being so privileged as to be loved infinitely by God.

St. Paul describes this work of the Holy Spirit: " . . . because the love of God has been poured into our hearts by the Holy Spirit which has been given us" (Rm 5:5). This is not merely an experience of being loved by God. The Spirit is the actual Love of God dwelling in our hearts. We carry this Love about us wherever we go. This Love is operating at all times, even when we sleep. The Spirit dominates our spirit as we seek that inner revolution of our mind to yield to God's Word through the Spirit's love.

This Word of God is a mighty two-edged sword that separates the soul from the spirit (Heb 4:12). No longer do we rely on our own powers to fulfill the command of Jesus whereby we and others know we are His true disciples. Sin has been put to death as we surrender ourselves to the indwelling Spirit. We replace ourselves as the center of reference with that of God's Spirit of love. As we experience deep down the Spirit as the love of God for us in Christ Jesus, that same Spirit brings forth His fruit and gifts so that we are turned outward towards others in love "because the love of Christ overwhelms us" (2 Co 5:14). Not only does the Spirit bring about a transformation in our consciousness that we are loved constantly by an infinitely loving God, but that same Holy Spirit is the loving energy that allows us to love others with His very own love.

We begin to live on a new level of being. We perceive ourselves in a new light. We walk in that inner dignity, all because of what Jesus Christ has done. "We are God's work of art, created in Christ Jesus to live the good life as from the beginning He had meant us to live it" (Ep 2:10). We perceive other human beings differently. It is not now with our "soul," our own human way, distorted by sin and ignorance of our true being in Christ, that we look upon others. We see the same world that we looked upon daily before but now we see "inside." We see that all others are loved infinitely by God, even though they might not have experienced that same Spirit of love within themselves. We understand that we really are one with them. They are our brothers and sisters and we are all parts of the Body of Christ. How can we hurt ourselves? How can we judge others who in their ignorance do not realize who they really are?

Love becomes, therefore, not something we strive to do. Love is the Spirit of God informing our spirit, the deepest levels of our consciousness, with the unifying force of God's very own uncreated energies that unite us with God and with our neighbors as we seek to perform every thought, word and deed in the spirit of love. "Whatever you eat, whatever you drink, whatever you do at all, do it for the glory of God" (1 Co 10:31).

The greatest freeing of the Spirit is to free us from the fears and dark anxieties, the aggressive "charging" toward others to control and possess them as "things" and to allow us to love each person that we meet, not as God would love him or her, but to love all in the power of God's Spirit. That which is impossible to our human personality becomes possible through the Holy Spirit who fashions us into an image of the Image that is Jesus Christ. Rooted in the Spirit's faith, hope and love, we love in the free creativity of children of God. In hope we love others in God's eternal love for them which then brings about a freeing in them to become actually what we have loved in hope.

The Spirit is the creative, transforming power of God that is always uniting what is divided. We enter into that same creative power of God to call people into their true, transcendent selves in the freedom of the indwelling Spirit

who allows us to let go of our fashioning of the world according to our own image and to enter into God's
movement of free creation.

THE SIGN OF DISCIPLESHIP

The sign, Jesus said, that we are His disciples, that we
have a part in Him, that He and His Father would come
and dwell within us, is whether we love one another as He
has loved us. We are called into that freedom of children of
God to love all, even our enemies, as the only begotten Son
of God loved them. When we understand that this is not a
mere moral virtue, to love others as Jesus has loved them,
but that this is the freeing of ourselves so that our spirit is
submissive totally to God's Spirit, then we will be caught up
into the personalized Love of God, His Spirit, that lives
within us. True freedom is not license, to do whatever we
wish on a body or soul level. But it consists in total submission as our spirit conforms our body and soul
relationships to the authority of the Spirit.

And you too have been stamped with the seal of the Holy
Spirit of the Promise, the pledge of our inheritance which
brings freedom for those whom God has taken for His own,
to make His glory praised (Ep 1: 13-14).

ONE BODY, ONE SPIRIT

The Spirit brings about a oneness within myself,
submitting the body and soul to the spirit under His loving
authority. When two or three gather together in love, there
is Christ (Mt 18:20) but there is also His Spirit bringing us
into His risen and transforming presence. The Church

Christ is the greatest freeing presence of the Holy Spirit on the earth. What is effected in one person toward God's indwelling presence is also effected between two persons yielding to His loving energies. When we allow that Spirit to work in order to free the society of mankind from division and hatred and dissensions, then the myth of the tower of Babel is finished and replaced by the Pentecostal experience. The universal language of love breaks down the isolation of brother against brother, fellow human being against other human beings and *church* begins.

St. Paul's recipe for building church is:

> Bear with one another charitably, in complete selflessness, gentleness and patience. Do all you can to preserve the unity of the Spirit by the peace that binds you together. There is one Body, one Spirit, just as you were all called into one and the same hope when you were called. There is one Lord, one faith, one baptism, and one God who is Father of all, over all, through all and within all (Ep 4: 2-4).

The Church, for St. Paul, whether local or universal, was conceived of as the *koinonia,* the community of believers linked together by the Holy Spirit in a unity of faith, sacraments, especially Baptism and the Eucharist, and a loving submission of all to Spirit-guided teaching authority. As Paul stressed the Spirit as the revealer of the living Christ, informing the members as the Head of the whole Body, his accent became more developed along the lines of the community as identified with the physical, resurrected Body-Person, Jesus Christ. It is the godly life that the Spirit brings to the Body of Christ which keeps it from being a mere, moral aggregate of members who honor the past memory of their Founder, Jesus Christ. It is an institution; yet it is also a corporate life in Christ.

The Body of Christ, the Church, is not ontologically identical with the historical, now glorified, body of Christ. Yet St. Paul insists that there is a partial identity insofar as the Spirit infuses into the Christian the Divine Life that is identical with the Divine Life of the physical Christ. Although the Christians in Baptism, and more so in the Eucharist, come into contact with the same Divine Life, they retain their own individual, human personalities and life. In fact, this is the greatest freeing power of the Spirit: to recapitulate the whole universe back to the Father in His Son, Jesus.

> . . . because God wanted all perfection
> to be found in Him
> and all things to be reconciled through Him and for Him
> everything in heaven and everything on earth,
> when He made peace
> by His death on the cross (Col 1: 18-20).

Not only does the part exist for the whole, but the part reaches its uniqueness and meaningfulness only in living for the whole. That is God's plan from the beginning. God's love made manifest in Christ is living His glorified, resurrectional life in His members through His Spirit. We are His members and the Spirit distributes His gifts "so that the saints together make a unity in the work of service, building up the body of Christ" (Ep 4:12). Each person is important as he or she brings his or her proper gifts to put them under the guidance of the Spirit to build up the Body of Christ. In this work, the Spirit frees us from our isolation and sense of meaninglessness in the light of the world community of which the Church is now the inner leaven within the mass.

LIVING THE LOVE OF TRUTH

Jesus had promised that the work of the Holy Spirit coming upon the Church would be to be the Advocate or Helper (Jn 14:15-17). He would be the Teacher (Jn 14:25), teaching us all things. He would be the Witness, the Spirit of truth empowering us to witness to Jesus (Jn 15:26). He would come as Judge (Jn 16: 4-11), convicting the world of sin and righteousness and judgment. The Spirit was to be our Guide (Jn 16: 12-15). We cannot fail and fall into error since the Spirit will free us from such darkness by guiding us into all truth.

Living in the love of the truth (2 Th 2:11) is St. Paul's way of summarizing the ecclesiastical work of the Holy Spirit. In the words of C. Spicq, it is "living an authentic Christian life in an environment of love."[14] The truth that Jesus promised us that would set us free (Jn 8:32) is to live the truth that we are all one in Christ, loved eternally by the Father, by living in love. The Church of Christ is truly His Body, forming one Son of the Heavenly Father insofar as its members live the truth in love, seeking at each moment to yield to the inner freedom to which the Spirit is calling us. Thus He guides each individual person and the whole community together, the part and the whole, to act only and always out of love for God. Thus the more we, as individuals, love Christ in His Spirit through the love we show towards our neighbors, the more the whole Body of Christ becomes "full" of the love of Christ, loving His Body, which is the Church.

A CHRISTIFIED UNIVERSE

Through such individuals, christified by the Holy Spirit, Christ reaches the rest of mankind and touches the

material universe. According to the dynamic vision of the
Church in the writings of Teilhard de Chardin,[15] the
christified, new Israel is a "phylum of salvation" that
spreads its inner life and hyper-personalism in a movement
of greater consciousness, always ascending until the
completion of the Body in the *parousia*. We can, in conclusion to this chapter on the Holy Spirit and His freeing
power, affirm that it is Love, the Holy Spirit, that is the
"within" of things, the immanent force unifying all conscious beings, personalizing them and calling them into the
unique beings that God had always loved as He eternally
calls them into greater being through relationships with
others in love.

The freeing power of the Holy Spirit, His very being, is
to bring us through faith, hope and love to a perception of
the transfiguration process that is now going on throughout
the whole universe. The whole world together is groaning
before it comes alive in its fullness. The Holy Spirit is not
merely working in the hearts of Christians. He is working in
the hearts of all human beings that they may discover the
divine energies of God bathing the whole universe and
charging it with His infinite love. The Body of Christ is
being formed through the priestly ministry of each human
being made according to that Image and Likeness that is
Jesus Christ and it is being shaped and fashioned by all
things material.

Thus we human beings become a source of freeing
power of the Spirit as we witness by our lives to the inner,
loving presence of the Cosmic Christ within matter, yes,
within a cruel, dirty, filthy, crime-infested world. Yet it is
God's world. "God saw that it was good" (Gn 1:18). Under
the Spirit, Jesus Christ is evolving this universe into His
Body. He is moving it towards Omega of which He is, the

full culmination of Himself in all of His members, the total Son of God praising and adoring His Heavenly Father. "I am the Alpha and the Omega, says the Lord God, who is, who was, and who is to come, the Almighty" (Rv 1:8).

MAN—A RECONCILER OF THE WORLD

We are entrusted with the same freeing power of the Spirit that has set us free. We are called to become "reconcilers." St. Paul beautifully teaches us our dignity of working to bring the whole world into Christ:

> And for anyone who is in Christ, there is a new creation; the old creation has gone, and now the new one is here. It is all God's work. It was God who reconciled us to Himself through Christ and gave us the work of handing on this reconciliation. In other words, God in Christ was reconciling the world to Himself, not holding men's faults against them, and He has entrusted to us the news that they are reconciled. So we are ambassadors for Christ; it is as though God were appealing through us, and the appeal that we make in Christ's name is: be reconciled to God. For our sake God made the sinless one into sin, so that in Him we might become the goodness of God (2 Co 5: 17-21).

Rather than running away from the affairs of the world, its development and fulfillment, the Christians should lead the human race through the truth that the Spirit reveals of the unity of all things in Christ Jesus. Our hope in the resurrection is a hope also of the social and historical resurrection of the entire universe to be spiritualized by the loving, transformative work of the Spirit of Jesus in His members. Whatever we add to make this world a better world has a lasting effect on the entire process and aids to build the Body of Christ. This the Spirit teaches us and allows us to see the dignity of our banal work, our small contributions, be it only a cup of cold water to someone who is thirsty, to visit one in prison (Mt 25) when it is informed by His loving power.

The building up of the Body of Christ, the Church, is not the gathering of an elect Group of "saved people" out of the human race with the rest of creation, both human and sub-human, destined to destruction. The entire Body of Christ embraces the resurrected body of God's creation, evolving through history and brought to its completion with man's cooperation. Every action informed by the power of the Spirit of love brings the cosmos forward towards completion. The only action that holds the process back is our own lack of cooperation with the Spirit through selfishness, fear and pride.

By contemplation given us by the Spirit, we can already "see" the power of the Risen Lord, which is the Holy Spirit, working in the lives of all men, regardless of what culture, religion, race or color. The Spirit calls us to become new wine skins to receive His new wine of love that will be able to ferment and we will adjust to its dynamic action within our lives. The Spirit fills us with Christian hope and optimism as He points out to us the Risen Christ working in a constant process of evolving through the basic goodness in all human beings made according to the image of God. He fills us with courage and eagerness to cooperate with His Spirit. As we toil painstakingly over the little plot of this universe entrusted to us at any given moment, we are buoyed up by the vision that God's material world has not been conceived by God to be destroyed but to be transfigured and brought into its fullness in and by the Spirit of the Risen Jesus

That is the great work of the Holy Spirit. He frees us to become the true persons God has always known us to be in His Son, Jesus Christ. He frees us from self-hate and insecurity, from all fears and anxieties, so that we can become the Risen Presence of Jesus in a world that has not yet heard the Good News: "I was dead and now I am to live forever and ever, and I hold the keys of death and of the underworld" (Rv 1: 18-19). The Spirit of Jesus frees us to become His loving presence to create others into ourselves, all parts of each other, so that we can enter into that eternal peace and joy, the ultimate fruit of the Spirit's love, realizing we are members of Christ. The Spirit's greatest gift is to make actual for all human beings, in a freeing process through contemplation, the truth of the Heavenly Father:

> You have stripped off your old behavior with your old self, and you have put on a new self which will progress towards true knowledge the more it is renewed in the image of its creator; and in that image there is no room for distinction between Greek and Jew, between the circumcised or the uncircumcised, or between barbarian and Scythian, slave and free man. There is only Christ: He is everything and He is in everything (Col 3: 9-11).

5

Freedom Through Contemplation

At 9.34 p.m., July 13, 1977, the entire city of New York in all its boroughs was suddenly plunged into darkness. With no electricity available for nearly an entire day, the city became a jungle. One resident called it "the night of the animals." Gangs of youth and later people of all ages broke store windows and looted millions of dollars of merchandise.

Psychologists tried to analyze the reason why, even in broad daylight, mobs of people joined in the looting, the most extensive in America's history. For many who had eyed goods through display windows but could not afford to buy them, it was a long-awaited opportunity. Doors and windows were smashed open. It was all there to be taken home, whatever one wanted. One psychologist could not bring himself to blame the looters, predominantly the poor who owned very little personal property. He claimed that all human beings have the potential of slipping readily out of the approved social system, controlled by sanctions and punishments, to follow a few leaders in obtaining what deep-down in their hearts they always wanted.

People at soccer games have turned into animals and killed each other as in a war. Under the power of war propaganda normal, law-abiding citizens and practicing

Christians can come to hate and to kill on sight the so-called enemy. Such mob psychology can be at work even in hysterical, religious meetings.

LOSS OF PERSONAL RESPONSIBILITY

Dr. Marie von Franz, a Jungian psychoanalyst, has pointed out how suggestibility increases enormously in crowds or groups because "in the group the sense of security increases and the feelings of responsibility decrease."[1] Our human freedom which we value so highly can be easily lost when we are placed in certain circumstances. In crowds especially, one's individual consciousness merges with the common emotion of the total group. The collective psyche, as Carl G. Jung has pointed out,[2] becomes more like the psyche of an animal. This is why mob psychology takes over. In the crowd one feels no responsiblity, but also no fear.

All of us have often felt this pull between an inner voice calling us to upright conduct that we realize we should follow and the pull of the crowd around us. All too often we yield to the outside crowd. The likes and dislikes, prejudices and hates of the society around us often control our attitudes and conduct. Are we really free?

Then when we look within our "hearts," the deeper levels of consciousness and of the unconscious, we must confess that there is a different "crowd" exerting powerful pressure to lessen our freedom of choice. All our past experiences exert their special power for good or evil within us. Sometimes in alert moments we can silence that inner "mob." But there are also moments when a seemingly more powerful force, from within me, takes over. Am I free?

St. Paul experienced this inner impulsion toward

actions he did not want to do. He confessed that he was "a slave to sin."

> In fact, this seems to be the rule, that every single time I want to do good it is something evil that comes to hand. In my inmost self I dearly love God's Law, but I can see that my body follows a different law that battles against the law which my reason dictates. This is what makes me a prisoner of that law of sin which lives inside my body. What a wretched man I am! Who will rescue me from this body doomed to death? Thanks be to God through Jesus Christ our Lord! (Rm 7:18-24).

We have seen how Jesus comes to free us from such interior "slavery." This is, however, a constant process of turning within and letting the Divine Physician enter into the inner areas of darkness with His freeing love. For the powers that have the greatest enslaving effect on our human free will are primarily not extrinsic to us but are rooted deeply in our psyche.

The early Fathers, through careful study of the inner working of their psyche, discivered that such inner promptings toward self-centeredness could be reduced to eight capital sins or passions. Evagrius of the fourth century writes:

> There are eight principal thoughts, from which all other thoughts stem. The first thought is of gluttony; the second, of fornication; the third, of love of money; the fourth, of discontent; the fifth, of anger; the sixth, of despondency; the seventh, of vainglory; the eighth, of pride. Whether these thoughts disturb the soul or not does not depend on us, but whether they linger in us or not and set passions in motion or not—does depend on us [3]

BANAL SINFULNESS

At times you must feel as I do, that even our sinfulness is not very exciting! Would that we could list our sinful tendencies so neatly that gluttony and lust and avarice etc. would show us the root of our sinfulness. But what an embarrassment not even to know in what our sinfulness consists! When we look into the murky darkness within our psyche, it would be consoling to see clearly-distinguished demons of anger, vainglory and pride raising their heads for the attack. But instead we see only vague phantoms, headless, squirming creatures within us making the picture of self-knowledge all so very unclear.

At times it comes down to an undefined feeling of meaninglessness in my life, a vague feeling of a wasted day, a year, a life. Then there are that boredom and ennui in prayer or at the Divine Liturgy that come over me. Or that quick resentment toward a neighbor, undefined, yet so lacking in love. Again it might be a seething violence of resistance to suggestions from others, a desire to withdraw in angry isolation.

St. Paul insists on a renewal of our minds, through an inner revolution (Ep 4:23-24).

Every thought is our prisoner, captured to be brought into obedience to Christ. Once you have given your complete obedience, we are prepared to punish any disobedience (2 Co 10:5-6).

NEPSIS

Such an inner discipline does not come to us easily or naturally. True self-knowledge of the psychic forces within us that are impediments to true, human freedom is a long process obtained through inner attention. This the early Greek Fathers of the desert called *nepsis*. It comes from the Greek word *nepo* which means to be sober, not inebriated. This is the inner vigilance that Jesus preached as obligatory if we were to awaken from our torpor and state of half-existing to become truly alive to His indwelling Spirit. "Watch you, therefore, and pray always . . . " (Lk 21:36; KJV).

Christians are to have a mental sobriety or balance, an internal disposition that puts them in the way of freedom to take their lives in hand and freely bring them into loving submission to the authority of Jesus Christ. Such inner attention brings the Christian away from any inordinate, slavish subordination to the senses or passions. It is more positively that complete openness of our total being to God's voice speaking within us. Such attention to the movements of the "heart" for the committed Christian is not a mere negative introspection but is a growing, positive openness and conscious response of his total, free being to God's invitation to grow in the likeness of Jesus Christ. "The pure in heart will see God" (Mt 5:8). Attention to what goes on in the consciousness of one's "heart" will bring about that inner cleansing "and then the vessel will also be clean on the outside" (Mt 23:26).

But how we squirm and will do almost anything to avoid this entering into the "heart," into levels of consciousness of not only our false *ego,* but also and more importantly of the true dignity to which we are called in Christ Jesus! Our modern world of technocracy is particularly suited to fill us with a variety of distractions that put off the real work of coming to know our true self and hence to enter into our true freedom, away from all other superficial pre-conditioning or sinful habits which bind us into a self-centeredness.

DRIVEN INTO THE DESERT

Jesus was driven into the desert by the Holy Spirit (Mk 1:12; Mt 4:1; Lk 4:1). This has been for Christians throughout all ages the model for "returning to one's true self," for entering into the heart and there doing the battle against the crippling, demonic forces that inhabit our interior psyche as well as the world around us.

The early Christians of the fourth century literally ran into the Egyptian and Syrian deserts with a zeal to do battle within themselves against the powers of darkness that impeded their full, free participation in the Resurrection of their Master, Jesus Christ.

And Christians, forever eager for the paschal victory, knew that true freedom came only through a prayerful attentiveness to their "hearts." This has been interpreted always by the image of an inner desert or wilderness into which the Spirit of Jesus drives the Christian ever deeper and deeper into fuller freedom.

When we have the courage to enter into the process of *metanoia,* the conversion or return to our true self, we begin to look honestly at our creatureliness, our "nothingness." This *nothingness* is beyond our own rational control. It is a gift which the Fathers of the desert called *penthos* (an abiding sense of our inner, creaturely poverty before the rich lovingness of God.[4] This is given to the *Anawim,* the *Remnant* of God's poor ones in spirit who dare to confront their non-being, their state of *nothingness* before God's *Allness.*

Psychologist William Kraft describes the state of

nothingness as speaking to man through the languages of
loneliness, aloneness, depression, anxiety, guilt, frustration,
anger, boredom, apathy and anguish.[5] Especially in a crisis
of limits middle-aged man

> . . . feels intensely his limits, emptiness and negativity; and
> the positive and fulfilling meaning in life is something
> distant, foreign, and almost unreal. He feels that he really
> does not matter much to anyone or to himself. He feels like
> a zero—a nothing.[6]

There can be many degrees of experiencing oneself as a
zero. Each stage of our religious development in our faith-
relationship with God brings its special pruning, darkness,
dying to the false self. This is another way of saying there
are different battles to be fought and different degrees of
freedom to be won as the crown of each battle. Basic to
most human development is the great temptation to avoid
the desert, to stop just short of this side where there is still
enough of everything, especially enough of self-power and
control. With the Israelites we wish to pitch our tents and
refuse to push on into the dark and forbidding unknown
that challenges our existence.

Thomas Merton well describes the unknown desert of
emptiness that demands so much in terms of dread:

> Following Gabriel Marcel, dread divests itself of the sense
> of possession, of having our being and our power to live, in
> order that we may simply be in perfect openness, turned
> inside out, of the defenselessness that is utter simplicity,
> and total gift. This is at once the heart of meditation and of
> liturgical sacrifice. It is the sign of the Spirit upon the
> chosen people of God, not the ones who 'have an inner life'
> nd deserve respect in the gatherings of an institution

notorious for piety but have simply surrendered to God in the desert of emptiness where He reveals His unutterable mercy, without condition and without explanation, in the mystery of love. Now we can understand that full maturity of spiritual life cannot be reached unless we first pass through dread, anguish, trouble, and fear that necessarily accompany the inner crises of spiritual death in which we finally abandon our attachment to our exterior self and surrender ourselves completely to Christ. But when this surrender has been truly made there is no longer place for fear and dread, no doubt or hesitation in the mind of one who is completely and finally resolved to seek nothing and do nothing but what is willed by Him, by God's love. [7]

A NEW AWAKENING

Today we are experiencing a great surge of interest in mind-expansion. There will always be the "camp-boys and girls," the dilettantes who dabble in instant mysticism. They too stay on the fringes of the desert but they have the illusion of having gone into themselves. They have never left the flesh-pots of Egypt. They are still enslaved to their false ego.

There are, however, in all walks of life, true, sincere seekers of the truth. They yearn for inner freedom. They hunger to find their true self in the Absolute Other. They are ready to face death in order to find true life. "God, you are my God, I am seeking you; my soul is thirsting for you, my flesh is longing for you" (Ps 63:1).

God can do anything with them for they have already seen that without God they have no meaning. They are ready to let the masks and false idols come crashing down as they move deeper and deeper into the inner battle. Such a person courageously puts the question to himself at each moment of his life and honestly waits for the answer to come back to him in silence: "Who am I really?"

With Gabriel Marcel he "has become once and for all a question for himself."[8] He is not afraid to reflect on his creaturely condition. He can stay "inside" himself groping for answers instead of running "outside" to be diverted from the important issue at stake. Marcel characterizes the sense of inner emptiness that comes to one who looks inside:

> When we are at rest, we find ourselves almost inevitably put in the presence of our own inner emptiness, and this very emptiness is in reality intolerable to us. But there is more, there is the fact that through this emptiness we inevitably become aware of the misery of our condition, a "condition so miserable," says Pascal, "that nothing can console us when we think about it carefully." Hence the necessity of diversion.[9]

This sense of emptiness is the beginning step toward a rich in-filling. The Christian takes the first steps into the wilds of the desert. He refuses to leave the battle but holds his ground and struggles in his heart to gain freedom from the many pre-conditionings of his past involvements in a life of sense indulgence, emotional and intellectual blindness. He stands stripped of any power. Broken and sick, he confronts God as the Ground of his being.

He rides into the levels of inner darkness and death as Albrecht Durer's knight in his engraving, "Knight, Death and the Devil."[10] The knight is in full armor riding through a valley accompanied by the figure *death* on one side, the *devil* on the other. Fearlessly, concentrating and with confidence he looks ahead. He is alone but not lonely. In his solitude he seems to participate in a power which gives him courage to affirm himself in spite of the presence of negativities of existence. Man going into his heart first discovers his aloneness. Faith springs into being as man discovers that he is not alone but in the depths of his being is the presence of the Almighty God. With Jeremiah he can cry out: "I never took pleasure in sitting in scoffers' company; with your hand on me I held myself aloof since you had filled me with indignation" (Jr 15:17). For in his aloneness he finds communion in his great need for the Transcendent God who alone can come to his rescue. In Him alone he places all his strength and aspirations. Poverty yields to His riches. Separation and loneliness dissolve into loving union with the indwelling God.

Meaninglessness and death, as shadows, struggle and die before the power of God's revealing light. God makes Himself present in the heart of man always creating man according to His very own image. True prayer is born in that moment in which man confesses his poverty and sinfulness and yet hungrily cries out in the totality of his being to receive the fullness of love and life that the Heavenly Father wishes to give him.

Inner freedom from meaninglessness comes to man as he yields in the deepest levels of his being to the creative love energies of the indwelling Trinity as God lovingly calls into his true nature of being His only begotten Son, Jesus Christ, through the loving presence of the Holy Spirit. God's action is one of "formation" of man, as His Son Jesus grows and matures within man's spiritual consciousness. The basic imageness according to which man has been created is experienced in prayer as a dynamic unfolding of the tremendous love-energies God has locked within him to become more and more in the "likeness" of Jesus.

CONTEMPLATION—TRANSFORMATION

In contemplation man moves from emptiness into the fullness of a child of God as St. Paul so beautifully prays:

> Out of His infinite glory, may He give you the power through His Spirit for your hidden self to grow strong, so that Christ may live in your hearts through faith, and then, planted in love and built on love, you will with all the saints have strength to grasp the breadth and the length, the height and the depth; until, knowing the love of Christ, which is beyond all knowledge, you are filled with the utter fullness of God (Ep 3: 16-19).

The contemplative, rooted in his remembrance of his basic nothingness, can rejoice in the experience of being loved so immensely by God in Christ Jesus. There can be no power of exploitation once he has remembered his "exile." In his reconciliation with the Father there can be only the humble, loving service of the Prodigal Son (Lk 15: 21-24). Prayer is now a state of ultimate submission to the love of the Father. The person of such liberating prayer brings his new God-consciousness into each event of his human existence. Indeed, he feels truly as though he had been lost and now has been found; he was dead and now he is alive (Lk 15: 24).

Each moment brings him into the raw stuff which he can now transform into occasions of reaching new levels of his inner dignity as a beloved son of so loving a Father. Each person whom he encounters, each event, each moment and each place provides him with relationships where in he can actualize his newly acquired consciousness of a beloved son of God. He springs alive in every relationship as he now has been awakened from the deep sleep of illusion that he was unlovable and that only power and attack would bring him a sense of identity. Contemplation beyond words and images, pretty speeches raised toward God in self-defense of his own insecurity, de-conditions him from his "normal" way of looking at reality. He has broken through his compulsive clinging to pre-conceived modes of thought, of interpreting reality through relational categories.

He is now open like a child to let God burst forth freshly in each surprising moment to show Himself in new and exciting ways of how much He loves man. Such a contemplative is freed from his ego-centered personality and now walks constantly in the light of God's pervading light.

THE ETERNAL NOW AND THE NOT YET

As one advances in contemplation, one also begins to breathe the air of freedom that can come only as a gift of the Holy Spirit. He learns his inner dignity to be an eternal love act of God that always was and always will be. He transcends time and begins to live in the *now* of God's unchanging holy love for him. As he experiences more deeply God's abiding presence and His energizing love within him, he learns how to give up all attachment to lesser desires and loves in order to love only God and to find in Him all other loves.

Christians like us should experience, as we meet God in our "heart," that deepest level of consciousness where God becomes the Source of our whole being, that we are most free in that awareness of God's infinite love for us. No power of the devil can touch this inner "holy of holies." No haunting memories from the past, no darkness of sinfulness can triumph over such an awareness. It is in such freedom that we learn how to worship the Father in spirit and in truth (Jn 4: 24).

It is the Holy Spirit who leads us into this inner dignity and allows us never to forget who we really are from all eternity in God's creating us in His Word. The Spirit divinizes us, making us participators of God's very own nature (2 P 1: 4). But this is not a static knowledge. The Spirit convinces us that we do not need the tactics of our past life to find ourselves but now He brings forth His fruit in life's actions, filling us with His fruit: " . . . love, joy, peace, patience, kindness, goodness, trustfulness, gentleness and self-control" (Ga 5: 22).

Part of this revelation by the Holy Spirit of your true identity in God's eternal *now* love for you individually is also His revelation that your neighbor and every other human being throughout the whole world has been made in that same image and likeness to Jesus Christ. You begin to experience a facility to turn to each person and love him or her with the Spirit's love. You contemplate others as the saints and angels do—in God's eternal love made manifest in Christ Jesus. Thus you can pierce through the false fronts that others leave behind or that your insecure false-self projected upon others. In direct and freely spontaneous love you give the love of God to all whom you meet.

God is no longer an object far away or a vague concept. He is a dynamic, creative force now loving and creating you and the whole world around you into "receptacles of God's goodness," in the words of St. Irenaeus. You know now that it is in a gentle receptivity to God's eternal, loving presence that you wait for Him, resting in His all-pervading love. St. Symeon, the New Theologian (†1022) beautifully expresses this contemplative awareness of God's eternal now presence in all things:

And he adores Him and is united always with the Light that
never sets,
the Light without the darkness of evening, the unap-
proachable Light,
which never leaves him, never completely wanders far from
him,
day or night, whether he eats or drinks,
not even in his sleep or on the road or in moving from place
to place.
And as he lives so he dies or rather even more clearly,
the Light is united with him completely in his soul eternally.
For how can the bride be separated from her spouse,
or the husband from his wife to whom he is once united?
So those who by repentance are united with God,
purify their souls in this world here . . .
Their cell is Heaven, they indeed are a sun
and the light is on them, the unsetting and divine light
which enlightens everyone who comes into the world.
It is made possible by the Holy Spirit.
In them there is no night; how, I cannot tell you.
For I quake even in writing these things to you and I
tremble
      in pondering over them . . . .
And so they live in their cells as in another nuptial chamber,
all lighted up and they think that they are living in Heaven,
or that they are truly living there; now see and don't doubt
it!
For they are not on this earth even if they are still held here,
but they live in the light of the future age,
in the light where the angels dwell
and where they move about . . .
O marvel! as angels and as sons of the Most High,
they will be after death gods united with God.
For He is God by nature; they are like to Him by adop-
tion.[11]

And yet, *not yet!* We are still contained in this bodily existence, joined to a world that groans together in travail "in one great act of giving birth" (Rm 8: 22). The tension of experiencing our inner beauty and dignity as children of God through the Holy Spirit (Rm 8: 15; Ga 4: 6) and seeing by reflection our daily response to our noble call and true identity already realized in God's eternal gaze of love fills us with a constant sense of humility and inner poverty. We cannot love others as we ought. Our reflection each day shows us how we have acted. We review in God the *not yet* situation and call out to Him for greater healing.

Interior tears flow at the realization of how far we are separated from our loving God. Like the Bride in the *Song of Songs,* we seek the Lord in our *not-yet* situation:

On my bed, at night, I sought him
whom my heart loves.
   sought but did not find him.
 .   I will seek him whom my heart loves.
 . . I sought but did not find him (Sg 3:1-2).

FREEDOM AND CONTEMPLATION—A GROWTH PROCESS

As we advance in prayer, we understand that our true progress consists in living within the dialectical tension of darkness and light, of God's absence and His returning presence, of our sinfulness and the Spirit's beautifying us so that we " . . . all grow brighter and brighter as we are turned into the image that we reflect" (2 Co 3: 18). The more we surrender to God's loving activity, the greater becomes our sharing in the freedom of Jesus.

Perfection can never consist in possession or in complacent, secure rest It consists, as St. Gregory of Nyssa in his *Life of Moses* points out, in a series of movements from darkness to light to luminous darkness. God is illimitable. Our hearts can never be satisfied with possessing Him through one level of attained, loving union. To be human, and, therefore, to be free, is to stretch out infinitely to love Him more and more.

Stability in possessing God through contemplation is the beginning of motion. Drinking of the living waters satisfies our thirst but also creates a new thirst. Freedom to surrender to God prompts us to go further in dying to self and thus become even freer.

Thus St. Gregory of Nyssa can write of this paradox between the dark and the light in the contemplation of God:

> And thus the soul moves ceaselessly upwards, always reviving its tension for its onward flight by means of the progress it has already realized. . . . For true vision of God consists rather in this, that the soul that looks up to God never ceases to desire Him.[12]

FROM THE CROSS TO GLORY

As Jesus discovered His full and perfect freedom only in freely surrendering His whole life to the Father, so too we enter into our freedom as children of God as we abandon ourselves to the Father's love. But surrender of self to God's free will to do with us whatever He wishes means a constant readiness to die to our own controlled lives. This is the Cross that St. Paul preached as a stumbling block to the Jews and the Gentiles (1 Co 1: 22-25).

As the Holy Spirit leads the Christian contemplative farther into the depths of his heart, the man of prayer reaches a spiritual maturity through deep infusion of the Spirit's gifts of faith, hope and love. He can live in darkness as well as in light, in God's presence as well as in His seeming absence. Nothing in life or death can ever separate him from the love of Christ Jesus (Rm 8: 38). No opinions of others, no persecution, no inner temptations towards any bodily, psychical or spiritual selfishness can take him away from God. He stands wonderfully *free*.

Like Lazarus, he stands breathing the fresh air like a man whose bonds have fallen from his limbs and he stands facing Jesus Christ and the world in a joyful freedom. He wants to shout the good news to all. "I die each day" (1 Co 15: 31) and yet he lives so powerfully as a new creature in Christ Jesus (2 Co 5: 17).

Through contemplating his life in Christ who leads him to the Father, he moves beyond the greatest fear: that of physical death, since the Spirit has led him into the very life of the Father. This is what St. Paul considers true *immortality* and *incorruptibility,* not the lack of physical dissolution, but the eternal presence of God's life within him. Thus Jesus has truly conquered sin and death in man's members (Rm 9: 2).

This is the man made free by contemplating the length and breadth, height and depth of the love of Jesus Christ (Ep 3: 18). In every event, every thought, word and deed, he witnesses the freeing power of Jesus to take away all fear and loneliness, isolation and separation from the community of fellow human beings. Jesus is truly risen and the contemplative in prayer daily experiences a share in His paschal victory.

He shows the freeing power of contemplation by living toward each of his fellow human beings with a love that approximates more and more that which the Father has for us in His Image, Jesus. "We have passed out of death and into life, and of this we can be sure because we love our brothers" (1 Jn 3: 14).

Ultimately true human as well as divine freedom consists in the ability to give oneself in love to all who approach. As we experience in deep contemplation, in a continued dying-rising process from darkness to light, the presence of the loving Trinity bringing us into a unity, the more we are impelled by the Spirit of God's love to go out and love others in a community of self-giving persons. Freedom is God's gift that enables us to experience our true uniqueness by the unity experienced when we die to our selfishness.

The true test of authentic contemplation ultimately must be measured by the freedom we possess in loving universally all human persons and in humbly serving them. We truly become free by losing the enslavement to ourselves through selfishness in order by contemplation to give ourselves freely to become the slaves of Jesus Christ. As we experience, in prayer, that Jesus Christ, the Image of the Heavenly Father freely, gave Himself up for love of us by His death on the Cross (Ph 2: 10), so we, progressively by His Holy Spirit, can freely give ourselves to serve Him in love. This love and service are shown to each of our brothers and sisters. Freedom is living in the unity of love that we are all Christ's and He belongs totally to the Father.

Our freedom ultimately consists in being God's slaves, for we truly become divine children of God when we serve as the Divine Son of God freely served us. Only prayer taught us by the Holy Spirit in the abandonment of the desert of our hearts can lead us into such freedom.

You know that if you agree to serve and obey a master you become his slaves. You cannot be slaves of sin that leads to death and at the same time slaves of obedience that leads to righteousness. You were once slaves of sin, but thank God you submitted without reservation to the creed you were taught. You may have been freed from the slavery of sin, but only to become 'slaves' of righteousness. If I may use human terms to help your natural weakness: as once you put your bodies at the service of vice and immortality, so now you must put them at the service of righteousness for your sanctification. When you were slaves of sin, you felt no obligation to righteousness, and what did you get from this? Nothing but experiences that now make you blush, since that sort of behavior ends in death. Now, however, you have been set free from your sanctification and ending in eternal life. For the wage paid by sin is death; the present given by God is eternal life in Christ Jesus our Lord (Rm 6:16-23).

6

HEALING UNTO FREEDOM

One of the most touching scenes of the Gospel is that of Jesus weeping at the tomb of his friend, Lazarus. "see how much He loved him!" (Jn 11: 37). Jesus commands the bystanders to remove the stone. He prays briefly to His Heavenly Father a prayer of thanksgiving because the Father would hear and grant His petition. Then we have those powerful words uttered with the full authority of God and the tenderness of a beloved friend:

> When He had said this, He cried in a loud voice, 'Lazarus, here! Come out!' The dead man came out, his feet and hands bound with bands of stuff and a cloth round his face. Jesus said to them, 'Unbind him, let him go free' (Jn 11: 43-44).

We believe in the power of the Word of God. What Jesus did, as recorded in the Gospel, He continues to do to all who wish to accept Him as the God-Man, the Redeemer and Savior, the healing Lord. How like Lazarus all of us are bound. And Jesus unbinds us and frees us. He still performs His saving role of freeing us. " . . . you will learn the truth and the truth will make you free . . . So if the Son makes you free, you will be free indeed" (Jn 8: 32, 36).

Jesus literally set the captives free, in fulfillment of Isaiah's prophecy (Is 61: 1), when He healed the sick and broken, the diseased or mentally unbalanced, those caught up in selfishness and unlove. Nor did He consider those whom He healed as healthy only when their sins were forgiven or when their bodies were restored to physical health. Jesus came to give them life that they might have it more abundantly (Jn 10: 10). It was the whole man that Jesus loved and to whom He ministered His life.

And in this He brought us human beings the Good News, the Truth that would free us from all lack of health. The Good News is:

Yes, God loved the world so much
that He gave His only Son,
so that everyone who believes in Him may not be lost
but may have eternal life (Jn 3:16).

The full healing for all of us comes only through the illumination of our minds and hearts by the Spirit of Jesus who dies for love of us. When the Son of Man was lifted up, He became a freeing power for all of us of every kind of demonic possession or sickness. Jesus refers to Himself on the Cross as the serpent that Moses fashioned of bronze and raised on high. Everyone who was bitten by crawling serpents, looking upon the raised serpent of bronze, lived (Nb. 21: 4-9).

. . . and the Son of Man must be lifted up
as Moses lifted up the serpent in the desert,
so that everyone who believes may have eternal life in Him
(Jn 3: 13-14).

LOVE HEALS

In our brokenness, when we are not in God's life, living fully in the *likeness* of His Son; we are outside God's

Kingdom. Just as Jesus preached the Good News that the Kingdom was breaking in upon each person who would receive Him as his Savior and Healer, so He touches us in prayer and leads us into the Kingdom relationship with His Father. Jesus still heals all who open themselves to His love which is the "imaged" love of our very Heavenly Father as Jesus teaches: "As the Father has loved me, so I have loved you" (Jn 15: 9).

What wonderful consolation to know by His Spirit that both He and the Father have come and made their home within us (Jn 14: 23). This is what the Kingdom of God is all about. God's eternal love, personalized in the intimate relations of Father, Son and Holy Spirit, touching us in that inter-communication that we call *prayer,* draws us out of our isolation and impersonal loneliness to enter into the very family of God. In such moments of prayerful communion with God within us, the power of sin and death is broken. Jesus truly lives and walks into our lives, the same, but now gloriously Risen Lord, and performs the same signs announcing the Kingdom of God.

> I am the resurrection.
> If anyone believes in Me, even though he dies he will live,
> and whoever lives and believes in Me
> will never die.
> Do you believe this? (Jn 11: 25-26).

Jesus still asks us this question. Do we really believe that He is the imaged love of the Father? Do we believe He can heal us and bring us into full health as He did all those whom He encountered during His lifetime, provided only they believed in Him? Or perhaps the more fundamental, urgent question is: Are we aware that we are sick and desperately need healing? Do we realize we are not living according to our full potential, the full life that God created us to enjoy and with which to praise and glorify Him?

William of St. Thierry in the twelfth century wrote in his treatise: *On the Solitary Life:*

> Although in sinning, (human) nature rejected order, and departed from the integrity of its original state, if it turns back towards God, it will recover immediately, according to the measure of fear and love it shows Him, all it had lost in turning away from Him. How agreeable it would be, and in principle how easy, to live according to nature, if only our foolishness would allow us to do so. Cure man of his folly, and immediately his nature would be able to look on the things of Nature without fear. [1]

We were created by God to be whole persons, totally integrated in all body, soul and spirit levels of relationships. Man found his relationship to the godly within him insofar as he had a mind, an intellect and will, to know and receive God's great love for him. When man, as planned by God in the first Adam and actualized in Jesus, the *New Adam,* lived according to his nature, freely consenting to love God in loving service, he was in harmony with himself (he was in *health*), with God and with the whole world around him.

But sin brought death to the God-life in man. He was plunged into a disorientation from God. Evil is not an objective entity existing by itself. It is an illusion of what man in sin was never meant to be. It is an unreal condition that man now assumes to be his true nature.

St. Gregory of Nyssa describes the condition of man who lives in sin:

> The lofty has been brought low; what was made in the image of heaven has been reduced to earth; he who was ordained to rule has been enslaved; what was created for immortality has been destroyed by death; . . . he who was

familiar with impassibility has been transformed into a life
of passion and death . . .[2]

BODILY NEEDS

All of us can usually detect when we are in need of
physical healing. The body is an organic mechanism. Parts
deteriorate. Viruses attack and bring infection into the
bloodstream. Vitality slows down as we grow older. Our
senses diminish in strength. Our vision and hearing usually
grow weaker as we advance beyond middle age. And so our
aches and pains cry out for a freeing healing, a restoration
to former strength.

We must believe that God is interested in our bodily
health. Jesus came as God's image in human form.
Wherever He went, He healed those sick and maimed in the
body. He never turned away the blind, the lame, the
crippled, the lepers and paralytics but He healed all who
believed in His power to set them free from their physical
slavery to bodily sickness and disease.

He went round the whole of Galilee teaching in their
synagogues, proclaiming the Good News of the kingdom an
curing all kinds of diseases and sickness among the people.
His fame spread throughout Syria, and those who were
suffering from diseases and painful complaints of one kind
or another, the possessed, epileptics, the paralyzed, were all
brought to Him, and He cured them (Mt 4: 23-24; Mt 9:
35).

This same Jesus, risen in glory, still brings His healing
love to mend our broken bodies. It is not that He sees the
body as something distinct from one's soul or spirit. As in
His lifetime, so now, Jesus, the Image of the loving Father, is

filled with love and compassion for all of us not freed from
sickness and disease of any kind. He sees us as whole persons
with very particular bodily needs.

PSYCHIC HEALING

Yet Jesus, the Divine Physician, knows better than our
modern doctors how the body, soul and spirit interact in us.
These are not tightly concealed compartments of self-
contained entities. About 70 to 80% of our physical diseases
are rooted in psychic suggestions received into the unconscious until the consciousness uses our autonomic system
to create the sickness that "acts" out the inner psychic
suggestion accepted. We all have daily experience of the
increasing stresses and anxieties that we must live under and
we know how such psychic factors powerfully affect our
bodies. High blood pressure, heart conditions, ulcers,
allergies, arthritis, even stages of cancer development[3] show
a direct relationship between a disturbed psyche and certain
somatic diseases and illnesses.

Scientists have shown that our minds are capable of
producing great electromagnetic energy fields which influence the human, bodily organism as well as other living
organisms: plants, animals. Experiments have been con-
ducted in Yoga, Zen Buddhism, TM meditation, Silva
Mind-Control, hypnosis and biofeedback that have shown
conclusively how mental activities can produce great
changes in the physiological state.

God has revealed much about the workings of the
human psyche through the discoveries made in depth-
psychology and psychotherapy. One of Carl Jung's com-
mentators, Dr. Ira Progoff, compares the psyche to a cross-
sectional drawing of geologic rock formation. At the top is a

thin layer of surface rock that we call consciousness. Below this is a thicker layer of rock that we call personal unconscious. Underlying both of these layers there is a dark, volcanic base extending back to the very core of the earth itself, bringing the individual into primordial contact with all of creation as a part to the whole. This Jung calls the collective unconscious or conscience of the Universal Man. Occasionally out of this volcano there erupt materials that rise to the surface, passing through the other layers.[4]

If a man is to attain an integrated personality, to harmonize all the various levels of psychic life within his mind (Jung calls this process "individuation"), the upper layers of the psyche must be harmonized with the lower layers. This means that the lower layers must be opened up to the scrutiny of the consciousness. Man will always remain crippled psychically and a victim of primordial factors in his life unless he opens up these lower layers to inner healing.

PSYCHIC BROKENNESS

When we allow ourselves in moments of deep relaxation and inner silence to go within and see what lies beyond the superficial level of our controlled consciousness, which Carl Jung calls the area, in fact, of the unconscious, we find an inner psychic world crying out for healing and harmony. Society with its "proper" way that we should act in certain circumstances, not doing some things just because it is not the agreed custom, does help us in this external control. But beneath this "properness," all too often we find a seething volcano of self-love, hatred towards certain individuals, readiness to use violence to get our own way. The jungle is very much within us underneath the external polish of an educated person. *The Lord of the Flies* is experienced by all of us if we have any self-knowledge at all.

FEAR OF FEAR

One of the greatest psychic enslavements is fear. It is the opposite of faith that pours into our spirit as a gift of God's Spirit of love. When we lack such a healing experience of God's personal love for us, we lack a sense of true identity. Fear is primarily centered in the apprehension of a future danger, unhappiness, doubt, anxiety, worry, dread, hatred, anger, horror, fright or terror. The thought of such impending evil weighs heavily upon our psyche and our body, crippling our growth, breaking down our health.

Fear can be about innumerable objects. It is the state of fear from which we must be delivered, for often the objects that we fear are only in our minds. The nation's number one health problem lies in the area not of mere bodily diseases but rather in the area of emotional and mental illnesses. And most of these psychic disturbances are due to needless fear. Most doctors are concerned with bringing a healing to the effects of fear. But we must discover the root of fear which is so often centered in a lack of faith and trust in God's loving care for us.

FEAR NOT

How often Jesus spoke words of confidence and loving strength to those burdened with fear. To the frightened disciples locked up in the Upper Room after His death He uttered these fear-dissolving words: "Peace be with you! . . . Why are you so agitated, and why are these doubts rising in your hearts?" (Lk 24: 37-38). On the stormy lake, Jesus asked the same disciples: "Why are you so frightened, you men of little faith?" (Mt 8: 26). He told all who were laboring under the heavy weight of any fear and were overburdened that He would give them rest (Mt 1.

Above all, He came to reveal to us that we hav~ a loving Father who numbers every hair on our heads. We are not to worry in the light of this great revelation, for if God takes care of the birds of the air and clothes the lilies of the fields, how much more, Jesus insists, will our Father in Heaven take care of all future needs? The conclusion is, therefore: "There is no need to be afraid, little flock, for it has pleased your Father to give you the kingdom" (Lk 12: 32).

We say, "Yes, Lord, I believe," yet we then begin to fear new areas of the unknown. This cripples us, preventing us from living dynamic, decisive lives because we are stalemated into a no-decision attitude. We wait for others to move us into positions where all freedom to make determined decisions is taken away. Or at least we find the field of choices narrowed down by our fearful inactivity. Such slavery removes us from the full life Jesus came to bring us.

One author describes the devastating effects of fear on us:

> For example, our mothers stamp fear upon us before we are born, and continue to do it after we are born, and until we have grown old enough to fear for ourselves. They create disease for us through their fears of diseases until we get old enough to create our own diseases. And that wretched fear follows us from the cradle to the grave. We are afraid we shall not succeed in business, and we create our own failures. We are afraid we shall not have the money to pay our bills for the current month and we generally lack something because we have created that lack. We fear bad luck, disaster and death, and it is a wonder that man has not swept himself off the face of the earth through his fearful creations. The offspring of fear are the creatures and

creations of this objective mind, and the subjective mind which is within objective mind accepts the unfortunate creations, believes the misrepresentations, and unites its own forces with those of the objective mind in bringing the pictured calamities into real external existence.[5]

Not only do we wallow in our own personal fears, but cosmic fears rise up and haunt us with nightmarish possibilities of nuclear explosions capable of destroying all life on this planet. We live in fear of the Soviets and the Chinese. And they, in turn, fear us. Earthquakes, tornadoes, droughts, epidemics that wipe out thousands of human lives are very real to us through rapid news coverage, filling us with unconscious fears that such cataclysms will soon befall us. Fear breeds fear. All too often our fears are fears of fear itself.

We must seek the causes of fear and then bravely eliminate fear by firm, rational action. We become liberated from the bondage of fear when we can look at the fear itself in terms of not only our own strength but the strength of God. If the fear has come from our own consciousness or unconsciousness, it will be dissolved by pouring into those psychic areas the healing power of God's vision of reality to dispel the projections of the insecure false *ego*. But the great question is: Are we ready and willing to let go of these fears that allow us an enslaving "comfort" and security instead of pushing into the dark world of deeper faith? To let go of such fears is a true dying process that many of us are not quite ready to make. That is to say, many of us prefer living in the cave of fearful shadows brought about by self-centered projections instead of surrendering in child-like faith to God, our Heavenly Father.

FEAR SPAWNS OTHER DEMONS

The giants of the Christian search for inner freedom, the Fathers of the desert, listed other demons spawned by fear, the living in the world of illision. Who can adequately describe the enslavement of worries that are born out of fear, anxiety, dread or regret? How crippling is anger that bursts out in violent verbal or even physical attacks against others or is allowed to eat away our inner integration through repression? Anger with its levels of rage, fury, irritation, revenge, jealousy, envy and scorn is one of the most enslaving signs of the false ego to seek power and domination over others.

Fear of what others may think of us holds us in its captivity, draining us of our ability to communicate in freedom and love with others. We react through an inferiority complex, a sick, wishy-washy yielding to stronger personalities or the inevitability of circumstances. We destroy the reputation of others by sharp criticism, spreading gossip, calumnies and slanders.

An inordinate desire for approval and praise from others fills us with vanity and crippling pride. We resort to lies, cheating, playing roles, all to create an impression which deep down we know is untrue.

Hatred is a strong emotion that is the opposite of love. It is indeed rooted in fear for we hate what we fear. We hate those who threaten us. It is the most destructive of human communication and growth into true humanity. All hatred is disruptive of communion in love. Therefore it is what most isolates man from fellow-man. It can only be dissolved by forgiving love. Jesus taught us that we are to forgive and to love even our enemies, those who hate us and seek to do evil to us (Lk 6: 27-35).

SIN AND GUILT

Dr. Karl Menninger once thought that sin with its accompanying guilt was a myth from an unenlightened age. He changed his mind after years of directing the very famous clinic for mental health that bears his name. In his well-known book: *Whatever Became of Sin?*, he points out that all of our human acts partake of some voluntary as well as involuntary choosing. True mental health, he insists, demands that we achieve as much responsibility as possible in our acts.[6]

Then there is the "feeling" of guilt through a legalistic code of morality that comes from past sins of impurity, of thought, of omission. Scrupulosity is a true prison and destroyer of both mental and physical health. The list of reasons for false guilt, fear of past transgressions, objectively true or subjectively "felt" as sinful is unending.

Even in doing good works, in loving others, subtle guilt can gnaw away at our spiritual and bodily health. Deep down in our state of sin, by not living in the fruit of the redemption of the glorified Jesus in His Spirit of love, we are mercilessly held in captivity to our own selfish projections.

With St. Paul we can cry out:

What a wretched man I am. Who will rescue me from this body doomed to death? Thanks be to God through Jesus Christ our Lord! (Rm 7:24).

JESUS, THE DIVINE PHYSICIAN

The Gospels were written to move us to believe that in Jesus Christ a new creation is possible. There is hope for all us because of Him Paul Tillich describes well this faith in the ability of Jesus to heal us as He healed all the sick who believed in Him during His life time:

> But faith means being grasped by a power that is greater than we are, a power that shakes us and turns us, and transforms us and heals us. Surrender to this power is faith. The people whom Jesus could heal and can heal are those who did and do this self-surrender to the healing power in Him. They surrendered their persons, split, contradicting themselves, disgusted and despairing about themselves, hateful of themselves and therefore hostile towards everybody else; afraid of life, burdened with guilt feelings, accusing and excusing themselves, fleeing from others into loneliness, fleeing from themselves to others, trying finally to escape from the threats of existence into the painful and deceptive safety of mental and bodily disease. As such beings they surrendered to Jesus and this surrender is what we call faith . . . We belong to these people, if we are grasped by the new reality which has appeared in Him. We *have* His healing power ourselves.[7]

Jesus stretched out His hands of healing and the sick felt the love of God pour into their broken bodies, minds and hearts. He was the Son of God and they, for a brief moment, hung suspended between the darkness of their own isolation and the light of the truth that they too were sons of God. They yielded to the presence of Jesus' love in their lives and they felt wholeness come over then.

That same Jesus wishes to pour out His Spirit of love into our hearts, if we only consent to receive this love. He wishes to heal us on the deepest level of our being, our spirit, by giving us *faith* to let go of all our fears and guilt and all the "unnatural" reactions that follow and to live in His new vision. It is a vision that makes us experience in the deepest levels of consciousness that we are all children of God, therefore, loved infinitely by God as He loves us in His only begotten Son. If God, therefore, so loves us, we ought to love one another ought to be the Christian conclusion. The Spirit of Jesus living in us gives us the healing power to love each person with God's love. We are liberated from our own projections. We truly stop and get off the world that we have falsely been creating.

HEALING OF THE SPIRIT

How can we enter into such a radical healing that goes so far beyond our little back aches and moods of depression but yet includes all of these? The first step, as we tried to point out, was to be able to look at ourselves on all levels of brokenness. This means a sincere readiness to go beyond the level of controlled consciousness and to enter into the nine-tenths of our *real* selves to get at the sources of our false, self-asserting ego.

Carl Jung in 1932 wrote a statement that loses nothing of its force and truth for the many years that have passed since then.

During the past 30 years, people from all the civilized countries of the earth have consulted me . . . Among my patients in the second half of life—that is to say, over thirty-five, there has not been one whose problem in the last resort was not that of finding a religious outlook on life. It is safe to say that every one of them fell ill because he had lost that which the living religions of every age have given to their followers, and none of them has been really healed who has not regained this religious outlook.[8]

We need a healthy disgust for ourselves, a nostalgia such as the Prodigal Son experienced as he fed the swine and pondered his separation from his loving Father. Convinced that we are living in an unreal world, we then cry out for a healing reconciliation between ourselves and God, with our neighbor and the whole material world around us. "I will leave this place and go to my father and say: Father, I have sinned against heaven and against you; I no longer deserve to be called your son" (Lk 15: 18).

Tears of true repentance pour out, like soft rain falling on the hard earth to soften it. The shell around our false world splits and God's penetrating love filters into our hearts to stir the great potential lying there into new life.

Such healing must be an on-going process of continually meeting God's love in prayerful communion. What has developed over so many years of self-centered living, as though the world revolved around ourselves, cannot be healed in one moment. It is only God's love, His uncreated energies touching us and calling us into the sonship of His Son, Jesus, that truly heals. How do we dispose ourselves to receive the gift of His healing love?

BE STILL AND KNOW I AM GOD

To enter into one's inner being, one must embrace silence. This is more than a mere refraining from speaking. It is an inward movement into what Scripture calls the "heart" of man. It is going beyond the controlled knowledge we entertain of ourselves and the world around us. And yet, how we resist this silencing of our own urge to create a world based on our selfish projections! We will do almost anything to remain "up" on top, in command of our lives by means of our intellectual powers. Given any situation, we have the power to fashion it by our minds according to our own liking. We can truly create whatever world we want, depending on our psychic needs. And yet how sadly we mistakenly call this our "creative" power!

It is in reality our power for undoing ourselves and putting off the whole process of becoming a healed, wholly integrated person, the one that corresponds to the name and person God knows us to be when from the depths of our being He calls us by our name (Is 43: 1). We are masters at avoiding a confrontation with the real person that we are. We play games, put on masks, become distracted by words and values that people around us live by. We can even busy ourselves "saying" prayers or talking busily to God in a dialogue whose script we have written. Yet we refuse in real silence, poverty of spirit, to look at our inner feelings, seeing both the light and the darkness that are struggling for possession of us. We fear to look inwardly and honestly, with purity of heart, to ask for healing from the Transcendent God when we see through genuine self-knowledge what needs to be sacrificed, what needs to be transformed.

Of all God's creations man has been made "according to God's image and likeness" (Gn 1: 26). Deep down at the core of man's innermost being is found the focal point where man can meet God in true healing love that Holy Scripture calls man's heart. It is in this "place" that Jesus tells us we are to go and adore our Heavenly Father:

> But when you pray, go to your private room and, when you have shut your door, pray to your Father who is in that secret place, and your Father who sees all that is done in secret will reward you (Mt 6:6).

We all too often dwell upon the negative parts of our personalities, usually the "persona," that superficial self in contact with the phenomenal order. We fail in deep, interior prayer, to allow the Spirit of God to flood us with the ontological realization that before God, in His reality and truth, we are already beautiful. There is an innermost self that is wholesome and healthy, full of God's very own life. Dr. Carl Rogers describes the movement away from our "exterior" self to the inner person:

> They move toward being persons who accept and even enjoy their own feelings, who value and trust the deeper layers of their nature, who find strength in being their own uniqueness, who live by values they experience. This learning, this movement, enables them to live as more individuated, more creative, more responsive, and more responsible persons. [9]

CENTERING PRAYER

Various words have been used by persons who practice and teach ways of making contact with one's deeper self. Transcendental Meditation is one description of a technique using Hindu meditation techniques made famous by Maharishi Mahesh Yogi. Most of the Far Eastern religions, including Zen Buddhism, have similar meditation techniques. Silva Mind-Control and a host of other mind-expanding systems, along with hypnosis, use similar methods of breaking one's habitually controlled level of conscious brain-wave activity to enter into a relaxed, more total in-touch with one's deeper parts. For some Christian groups, usually among Protestants that favor developing the inner powers of the psyche through meditation, the term *metaphysical* is used.

For Eastern Christians, who inherited the *hesychastic* type of prayer from the Desert Fathers, [11] a centering process is used that employs the Christian *mantra* of the Jesus Prayer. The "heart" is opened up to the healing power of the indwelling Trinity.

Whatever technique is used, we must always realize that it is in a faith vision that we wish to be centered so as to receive God's loving energies, and, surrendering to them, we may find deep healing. Such opening of the psyche, especially of layers of the unconscious, can be extremely dangerous. Instead of healing, we can release the demonic and fall into great fears and guilt. [12] Repressed material that has been drowned in the unconscious can rear threateningly to disturb one in prayer. Sexual feelings can arise, even influencing the whole body. The strange faces of the demonic flash now brilliantly, now darkly from within. The many fears, anxieties, moods of anger, depression and hatred that come upon us from no apparent outside cause are indications of a smoldering volcano lying deep beneath the surface of our habitual knowledge of self. But this is precisely why we need a strong faith vision of God's presence. We can then consciously place all such disturbances under His healing love.

As the spirit moves into a harmony with God's Spirit, we feel great loving energies uniting us with God, with our neighbor and the entire world. The walls of defensiveness that we built up, the aggressive moods of attack to preserve our false identity, dissolve before God's love and our newfound sense of oneness with all of the universe. We feel ourselves entering into a new integration of spirit, soul and body. By such daily prayer we can release great powers of inner healing that will flow over our psyche and even our body, bringing healing and new strength.

As we yield to the indwelling Trinity and allow ourselves to be loved, we experience a movement into new freedom as children of God, loved infinitely by God Himself in Christ Jesus through His Spirit. Our potential for *being* expands into a realized consciousness. We are being healed! The inner transformation that St. Paul speaks about (Ep 4:23-24), is experienced as now taking place. Unsuspected powers to love, to-be-towards God in total surrendering oblation, towards ourselves in a healthy self-love, towards others, open up slowly. How exciting to feel the healing power of God's love dissolve the tight bonds of enslavery from so much of the past, from so much that we never even realized could have been a source of non-life in us.

MEDITATION—HEALING

To enter into the psychic silence that allows us to receive God's Speech of Love, Jesus, indwelling us through His Spirit, there can be certain methods, provided we understand that the methods are geared to the release of the Spirit to replace our own aggressive projections. There are various levels of psychic silencing of the emotions, the imagination, the memory, the intellect and the will. But the greatest silence, when we have reached that inner "still point," is when our spirit is united with God's Spirit. Then "heart speaks to heart" in silence that is the language of self-surrendering love.

Most of us Westerners all too readily jump into prayer by using immediately our reasoning powers while ignoring our bodies and how they are situated within the context of a given place and time. We need to place ourselves in a position of physical quiet and harmony. The body with all of its nerves, muscles and organs must be brought into a relaxed "wholeness." For this we should choose a very relaxed position, either sitting or standing. Most people relax best when sitting down. Some more athletic persons can attain great relaxation through sitting in the lotus position or semi-lotus, in which the legs are crossed as one sits on a cushion with spine up straight. Most can attain a bodily relaxation by sitting on a straight chair in such a way that the spinal cord is straight up and down with no hunching of the shoulders.

Proper breathing is important in attaining an inner state of relaxation. Breathing diaphragmatically puts us into an inner rhythm that allows the body to move into a submission to the soul-powers. To breathe in this fashion, one inhales and becomes aware of the diaphragm muscle in the abdominal cavity extending outwardly. As one exhales, the diaphragm moves toward the spine. Back and forth in such oppositional breathing, one feels himself sinking into a state of great physical and psychic relaxation. He is able to let his faith exercise itself on a larger level of receptivity to God's movement. He is now *listening* to God and giving Him the freedom to speak His Word when and how He wishes.

After consciously attending to removing all tension from the entire body, we then can move into a method of "descending" into the deeper levels of our being. In Ira Progoff's *Process Meditation,* he allows the meditator to read slowly or have him listen to the reading of such meditations that employ archetypes such as the well, the silencing of the waters and their clearing from the mud, the cathedral and the monk in the white robe.[13]

I like to suggest a descending movement where the meditator takes an imaginary elevator from the twentieth floor of a building down slowly to the basement. As the elevator passes each floor, he becomes more relaxed, lets go of all bodily and psychic tensions in order to arrive in deep faith before the Risen Lord. In His presence, the meditator fixates on a *mantra* or phrase of his own choosing that will keep him focused on the presence of Jesus or the Trinity, Father, Son and Spirit. It is when one feels completely one with the loving power of God, personalized and turned toward the meditator, that the latter begins to receive complete healing from God.

Thus the steps for such transcendent meditation unto inner healing, body, soul and spirit, are briefly these:

1. Select a quiet place, free from noise and interruptions. The best time is in early morning before the activities of the day or before meals but not after meals or when one is very fatigued.

2. Take a position that is comfortable yet disciplined enough to prevent sleep or undue distractions to arise. This can be sitting on a cushion on the floor or on a straight-back chair.

3. Localize yourself in the presence of the Trinity by making acts of faith, adoration, hope and love.

4. Begin to breathe consciously. Feel your breath entering into your lungs and follow slowly its exhalation. Synchronize your inhalation and exhalation with the opposite movement of your diaphragm. Lengthen your breathing into calm, long breaths. Feel yourself literally relaxing.

5. Consciously start from the head and go through all parts of the body, commanding each part to give up any tension and replace it with complete relaxation. Enjoy the feeling of becoming whole physically.

6. Descend by any technique that is meaningful and yields the best results, into your "heart," the deeper layers of your consciousness where beyond words and images you will meet God. I have described this suggested technique of going down an elevator above and in other works.[14]

7. The most important part of this healing exercise

consists in the deep faith that Jesus Christ is present and still healing all who truly believe in His healing love. It is imperative to approach the Divine Physician with that faith that He himself insisted upon:

> Have faith in God. I tell you solemnly, if anyone says to this mountain, 'Get up and throw yourself into the sea,' with no hesitation in his heart but believing that what he says will happen, it will be done for him. I tell you therefore: everything you ask and pray for, believe that you have it already, and it will be yours. And when you stand in prayer, forgive whatever you have against anybody, so that your Father in heaven may forgive your failing too (Mk 10: 22-25).

8. The first element in such healing through child-like faith consists in forgiving others any injury they may have caused us. Let go any animosity towards any other. Feel a oneness as the love of God's Spirit unites you with that person or persons.

9. The important and final step in such meditation for healing is: picture Jesus touching that area of the body, soul or spirit that needs healing. This might be a relationship with someone not present. See yourself already healed and living in a new-founded joyful love towards all others. Begin to thank. God for such a healing. Know it is already being done as you believe.

Agnes Sanford calls this process of picturing oneself already being healed "visualization." She describes it:

> Make a picture on your mind of your body well. Think especially of the part of the body that most needs to be well. See it well and perfect and shining with God's light. And give thanks that this is being accomplished.[15]

All true healing in meditation or any other form may focus upon a given need, be it a physical healing or some psychic area of inner healing or a spiritiual need. As we pray the prayer of faith and allow the healing power of God to pour over us, we move to a higher level of healing: that of the spirit. The Spirit of God allows us now to receive His in-pouring faith, hope and love so as to surrender our lives completely to God. New freedom, never so experienced, floods us as we now believe with fresh abandonment that God truly loves us, even when He disciplines us (Jn 15:1; Heb 12:5-13). We see with new eyes that all things work unto good to those who love the Lord (Rm 8:28).

Leaving such prayer, we should entertain a spirit of great gratitude, knowing that God has truly answered our prayer. We are healed! And for this we thank God all that day. We act on the conviction that God has heard the prayer and is progressively healing us, even though there may not be an instant manifestation.

HEALING IN A GROUP

People in all times throughout Christianity have been drawn to gather together in the name of Jesus to pray for favors, especially for healings for themselves and for others, present or absent (Mt 18:20). One of the exciting elements of the Charismatic Renewal is the renewed faith in the presence of the healing Lord when Christians gather together in child-like faith to pray for healings.[16]

In such a gathering, be it with two or three or a larger segment of a prayer group or a healing service where hundreds are in attendance, the important element is the sharing of a child-like faith that the Lord is present and wishes to heal all who believe. As the Spirit moves through the group, the spirit of all who attend is opened to deeper healing and in that proportion healing power flows through the individuals to effect healings of all kinds. One must caution against any undue hysteria in such large crowds where the "healer" or one who is conducting the healing service makes demands for instant manifestation of a healing. God will never meet our time schedule! Thus the group gives thanks for such presence of God and for the healing power experienced. But at the same time all concerned must be taught to continue such healing, both on an individual prayer level alone with God and in a group with others. It is not again so much that we doubt that God has answered our prayers and so we ask again, but it is more in a strengthening of our faith by thanking God and expecting a greater outpouring of healing.

The experience of being touched during a healing service can be a most important element of healing. Jesus used matter in His healings. He often gazed intently upon a sick person in need of healing. His usual technique, however, was to touch the sick. Touch is a most primal experience of being one with the other person who touches us. Healing effects that which touch acts out: we are really all one, parts and members of Christ's Body. We cannot really be separated except in an unhealthy way that comes from sin and death.

HEALING OF MEMORIES

This can be a very deep healing in the context of a group. A leader leads the group back into the past of the individuals suggesting periods of one's life when hurts developed, angry moods, resentment towards certain persons, poisoned relationships, unforgiveness festered the heart for many years, etc. Without any undue fear or guilt, each individual calls down the healing power of the Spirit of Jesus to touch this or that relationship or scarred memory and bring it into a new vision of love and forgiveness.

Deep healing of suppressed material can be effected as one in such group prayer sees his fragmentation and alienation from his true self in Christ and cries out for healing. The effectiveness depends upon the sincerity and faith that Jesus will truly heal such past hurts, hidden resentments or unforgiveness.[17]

SACRAMENTAL HEALING

Without entering into the healing power of the sacraments of Baptism and Confirmation, let us center upon the two most available sacraments for adults: the sacraments of Penance and Holy Eucharist. Among Catholics, Orthodox and Episcopalians, the sacrament of Penance or Reconciliation is a powerful healing of the inner recesses of one's consciousness and unconscious and a source of great growth in inner freedom. What needs to be emphasized in the reception of this sacrament is the necessity of the penitent to enter deeply into his being and expose his wounds in their root sources. Yet few of us have sufficient self-knowledge of the movements of our hearts to confess our need of healing in specific areas. The "grocery list" of sins that we found in a prayer book or memorized, routine confession after confession, kept our knowledge of self confined to external actions that never really allowed us to expose ourselves at deeper levels. It is no wonder that weekly or monthly confession over years yielded very little inner healing.

Erich Fromm, one of the leading contemporary

psychoanalysts, boldly makes the statement that "most of what people have in their conscious minds is fiction and delusion . . . therefore consciousness as such has no particular value." Karl Rahner insists strongly on deeper prayer in order that one can enter into greater freedom:

> No man can give himself the freedom he needs to respond totally to God. For this task he needs to be set free by God Himself, and he is set free only in prayer. Prayer then is the way, because it is the expression of human powerlessness, the affirmation of man's fundamental nothingness and the cutting off of all means of escape.[18]

In the Roman Rite there are many new possibilities of entering into a prayerful attitude in the new Ritual for the sacrament of Reconciliation. The stress is on a prayerful dialogue between the penitent and the priest, with a vivid presence of God through the reading of selections from Holy Scripture and encouragement given to spontaneous prayer. One helpful way to reach deeper inner healing is to make our self-accusations to the Heavenly Father in the name of Jesus and His Spirit, expressing not so much the violation of a law as true sorrow at a profound level of knowing the infinite love that God has for us and that we have freely turned away from His high calling as a loving child of God.

Agnes Sanford writes of her powerful experience the first time she ever received the healing sacrament of Penance:

> . . . I was flooded from head to foot with the most over-whelming vibrations. I felt a high ecstasy of spirit such as I had felt before when very spiritual people had prayed for me. I felt a deep inner burning which I had felt when

receiving a "healing treatment" from someone who had the faith to set free the healing power of God in prayer. I knew by the inner warmth and tingling that my nerves and glands were being healed of their overstrain and weakness. And indeed a healing process did begin in me at that time. But in addition to these manifestations of the grace of God through the forgiveness of Jesus Christ I felt something else that I cannot put into words. I can only say that I felt for the first time that Jesus loved me. Something touched my heart. A stream of tenderness was released within me. And I knew that this was the forgiveness of Jesus Christ—His life, given for me.[19]

THE BREAD OF LIFE

Jesus reached the peak of His emptying love for us human beings in the Last Supper and on the Cross. When He took bread and wine and, by the power of the Holy Spirit of love, gave Himself under those symbols of food and drink, He imaged most perfectly the self-giving love of our Father in Heaven. The Holy Eucharist is the new Covenant whereby God continually gives His blood for the remission of sins and the life of the world (Heb 9:15, 25-28).

In the Byzantine Liturgy the fruit of the Eucharist is described in the prayer of the priest before communicating: "May it be for the remission of sins, the forgiveness of offenses, the communion of the Holy Spirit, the inheritance of the heavenly kingdom, for confidence in You and not for judgment or damnation."

Jesus Himself tells us in the Last Supper: "drink all of you from this, for this is my blood, the blood of the covenant, which is to be poured out for many for the forgiveness of sins" (Mt 26:28). He comes to us as the Lamb of God who takes away our sins. Again it is dependent upon our faith and our desire to be touched deeply by the Lord and thus to be forgiven. We approach God, the consuming fire (Heb 12:29), with great expectancy that all the sins of our past will be wiped away, that the deep roots of sinfulness in us will be replaced with a new surgence of God's eternal, resurrectional life in us. Like the woman with a hemorrhage in the Gospel story (Lk 8:43-44), we need only touch Jesus and His power will flow into us bringing us new life.

I tell you most solemnly,
if you do not eat the flesh of the Son of Man
and drink His blood,
you will not have life in you.
Anyone who does eat My flesh and drink My blood
has eternal life,
and I shall raise him up on the last day.
For My flesh is real food
and My blood is real drink.
He who eats My flesh and drinks My blood
lives in Me
and I live in him.
As I, who am sent by the living Father,
Myself draw life from the Father,
so whoever eats Me will draw life from Me.
This is the bread come down from heaven;
not like the bread our ancestors ate:
they are dead,
but anyone who eats this bread will live for ever (Jn 6: 53-58).

EUCHARISTIC HEALING

Just as in the lifetime of Jesus, so in His Eucharistic

presence, He forgives us our sins by leading us through His Spirit into a new realization of our sonship with Him of the Heavenly Father. He removes the illusions under which we live and perceive ourselves, God and others. And in that infusion of deeper faith, hope and love, we find deep healing of body, soul and spirit. We touch Him, the Divine Physician, and He touches us. His divine life pours into us, bringing us a new share in His eternal life. Of all the sacraments, the Eucharist is the climax because here Jesus Christ, the perfect Image of the Father, gives us Himself unto eternal life. Here He conquers in that eternal *now* of self-immolation on the Cross for love of us individually all sin and death that exist within us. Even though we may be broken in body and still will die, yet we already live immortally in His divine life. Here we most experience a sharing in His glorious resurrection as His Spirit dissolves in us our lack of love for God and for neighbor. Immortality, the fruit of the healing power of Jesus in the Eucharist, is not that we shall never die physically, but it is the experience of living now in the risen life of Jesus. We are already in His Body. And the sign of the degree of this immortality is the love we have for our neighbors since the healing is that of conquering the separation of members from the Head, Jesus Christ, and the union of all the members with each other in His Spirit of love. The Church begins here in the Eucharist as we learn to live for the community, the *koinonia,* the Body of Christ. In the breaking of the bread, we recognize Christ in our fellow human beings, our brothers and sisters in Christ. We go forth healed in order to become a healing force for others, "reconcilers" of the world to Christ Jesus (2 Co 5:19).

GO, HEAL THE SICK

Jesus sends us forth from the Eucharist to bring His love to all whom we meet. We are to wash their feet, feed and clothe them, in a word, we are to let the love of His Spirit flow freely and extravagantly through us to others. We are to give away this new-found life and not bury it in the sands of our own self-centered heart. Healed of the separation from God and neighbor, we can now bring God's healing power to take away separation in the lives of others.

This is the great commission that Jesus gave His disciples and all of baptized in His name:

> Go out to the whole world; proclaim the Good News to all creation . . . These are the signs that will be associated with believers: in My name they will cast out devils; they will have the gift of tongues; they will pick up snakes in their hands and be unharmed should they drink deadly poison; they will lay their hands on the sick, who will recover (Mk 16: 16-18).

As the Acts of the Apostles is a running account of all the wonderful miracles and healings effected by the early believers of Jesus, so we are to bring such power of healing into our contemporary society. He still promises that if we remain in Him, we may ask anything of the Father and He will give it (Jn 15:7). Such Christians, healed of doubts and fears, who live in His light, believe what St. James wrote:

> But we must ask with faith, and no trace of doubt, because a person who has doubts is like the waves thrown up in the sea when the wind drives. That sort of person, in two minds, wavering between going different ways, must not expect that the Lord will give him anything (Jm 1: 6-8).

Jesus continues to heal the broken of the world through those who surrender their lives to Him. How humbling is the thought that God ties His healing gifts to our free cooperation to be His instrument to touch others and bring God's freeing love to them! His Body is being healed and completed through our cooperation. As we are healed and "apprehended" by Jesus Christ, to that degree will He use us to extend His healing love to all whom we encounter in a prayer of faith.

People in the Charismatic Renewal often pray that they may receive the gift of healing. There is a danger to objectivize or *thingafy* the gifts of the Holy Spirit and forget that the Spirit is the great Gift of the Father to us through Jesus. As we are healed of our blindness and sinfulness, surrendering more completely to the power of the Risen Jesus, the Spirit frees us to be open and gentle towards others. His love will pour more and more powerfully through our humble ministrations to the sick who labor on all levels of non-being.

We become more bold as we humbly recognize God's infinite love within us wishing to be poured out upon those who do not know Him yet as "Yahweh who heals" (Ex 15:27). We believe, when persons are open to receive God's love in us, that whenever we pray for another, either individually or in a group, there will always be a healing, at least of the spirit by a deeper faith as we humbly share God's gift of faith given to us. It is only love that heals. And true love is the uncreated energies of God poured out through purified hearts into the hearts of others. As fear, guilt, hatred and unforgiveness destroy health both in ourselves and in others whom we affect, so love of God alone is the power that binds up wounds and heals unto the wholeness planned eternally by God.

HEALING THE WORLD

As in deep prayer we have been freed of selfishness and fear by the infinite love of God made manifest in us by Jesus Christ, so we will become a transforming, healing love for all others that we meet. What a power for releasing the love of Jesus into this broken world we, as healed Christians, possess! But are we aware of this inner power that we carry into the asphalt jungles of our cities, the living cemeteries of the homes for the aged, into our schools, churches, homes, banks, on beaches and in theaters?

Living in New York and sensing so much violence, hatred, enfleshed evil all around, I often think that the reason why utter chaos does not break out is that there are prayerful people in this city releasing God's love as a healing rain to fall gently over the city in order to purify it of selfishness and to stir new life in the hearts of those not freed by an experience of God's personal love for them.

An exercise I am fond of doing, whenever I take a subway ride or drive a car in New York or come zooming over the big city in a plane, is consciously to let the love of Jesus use me as a point of becoming "inserted" again into the lives of so many people. I ask Jesus to cover them with the infinite love that His Father and the Father of us all has from all eternity for each of those millions of people.

It is especially in the deep quiet of night that the Christian can rise in adoration to release Jesus' love, not only in his city, but he can direct that released love toward any part of the world. War-torn areas, drought-lands where thousands suffer from a lack of water, hospitals where people are suffering and dying, prisoners behind bars or in concentration camps who seek the freeing power of the Savior, all these and more become the "target" for healing as the Christian in prayer believes, as a child, that Jesus still becomes present, not by a bodily presence, but by a presence of love, as he loves the world in Him.

A banner in my room has these words:

In loving one another,
God in us is made flesh.

True love for God brings forth an intense and strong love for others. Our reality and the degree of being a fulfilled human being consist in how present we are in loving service to how many persons. But this is another way of describing our own process of individuating healing and our ability to bring God's healing love to others.

We let go of our aggressive, attacking attitudes towards others. Much like St. Paul, we live an experience of a mother bringing the whole world into new life. The healing love of God within us "overwhelms us" and heals us of the illusion that we are strangers to those who are different from us. The same energizing, loving God, experienced within as Love and Life, is found by faith, hope and love in each creature that we meet. We do not so much bring Jesus into the world as we "unveil" Him who is the *Logos* according to whom the world has been created (Jn 1:2). In Him all of us live and move and have our being (Ac 17:28).

We do not bring healing to others so much as we dissolve in them, by the love of God in us, the non-being of sin, fear, guilt and hatred. We point out to them the inner beauty that is already theirs, yet in their darkness they fail to see it. The light of Christ shines through us to them, enlightening them to know they are loved and inviting them to return God's love and ours. That is why love alone heals because true health is ultimately possessing God's very own life which is love that brings all strangers into God's family and makes all of us one in the one Son of God. In Him, the whole Jesus Christ, is the Father praised and glorified forever.

7

Freedom Demands Discipline

It was my privilege to spend three summers on Mount Athos, the republic of Orthodox monks, on a 35-mile-long peninsula jutting into the Aegean Sea in northern Greece. My conversations with the hermits of Karoulia were the greatest inspiration of my visits. In their thirst for greater solitude, about twenty Greek and Russian monks lived in tiny huts, like eagles, on top of sheer rock, with the heavens above and the surging sea below. Most of Mount Athos is verdant, abounding in forests and springs.

At the southern-most tip of the peninsula there was nothing but a precipice of rock. Here were some of God's chosen athletes, ascetics who took St. Paul's words seriously to pray incessantly. They slept only a few hours, no more than four, and spent the other hours in prayer, usually reciting continuously the Jesus Prayer. They ate the hard left-over bread from the bigger monasteries; they soaked this in tea. There was no vegetation and no running water. They collected in cisterns the rain water that had to last them the entire year.

Here I found the exact asceticism that had been practised in the fourth and fifth centuries when the Egyptian desert became a "thebaid" of monks. Thousands had fled the pagan world so that they could take literally the Gospel in all its stark simplicity. Both for the monks of

145

the early centuries of Christianity and for those of Mount Athos their asceticism consisted of fierce vigils, fastings, mortifications, constant prayer, enduring the heat of summer and the terrifying cold winds of winter. I was quick to think at first that their asceticism was an exaggeration. My common sense seemed to tell me that God does not ask that much of us.

Yet the spirituality of such men, as St. Macarius the Great called them, men "intoxicated with God," shouts out to us the terrible jealousy of God who, after having given Himself so totally to us in His Son, Jesus, asks all from us. I found that their asceticism was not a form of pride, coming from a spiritual "athletism." Their terrifying self-discipline came from their great love for God. In prayer they had deeply experienced the warmth of God's love enkindling a similar warmth of a return of love in their hearts.

St. Bernard summarizes for all Christians of all centuries the focus of their lives:

> You wish me to tell you why and how God should be loved. My answer is that God Himself is the reason why He is to be loved. As for how He is to be loved, there is no limit to that love. [1]

Christians of earlier ages, distinguished for asceticism, understood clearly the end of their lives on their earth. Jesus Himself commands us to be perfect, even as our Father in Heaven is perfect (Mt 5:48). St. Paul also exhorts us: " . . . praying that you will never lapse but always hold perfectly and securely to the will of God" (Co. 4: 12-13). The need for discipline and the readiness to pay the price are dependent on the conviction of the importance of the goal desired. The Old Testament also commands us: "You must be entirely faithful to Yahweh your God" (Dt 18:13). Yahweh had commanded His People Israel in the desert to love Him with all their hearts, with all their souls and with all their strength (Dt 6:5).

Jesus Himself paraphrased this same command to be the summary of the end of our human life:

> You must love the Lord your God with all your heart, with all your soul, and with all your mind. This is the greatest and the first commandement. The second resembles it: You must love your neighbor as yourself. On these two commandments hang the whole Law, and the Prophets also (Mt 22:37-40).

The greatest thing that we human beings can accomplish in our lives, the supreme purpose of our lives, is to love God as perfectly as we can and to love our neighbor equally. Thus the Christian life does not primarily consist of difficult accomplishments achieved in an ascetical way. Perfection is not in fasting, vigils, sleeping on the earth. Neither does it consist in solitude nor even in great works of charity done to the poor. All of these acts can be important means to attain the one primary end: love of God and of neighbor. "If I give away all that I possess, piece by piece, and if I even let them take my body to burn it, but am without love, it will do me no good whatever" (1 Co 13: 3).

The goal of our life is to enter into a union of will through love with God that is proved by our love for others. Certain attitudes and actions will follow upon this central principle. Understanding the supreme goodness and greatness of God, His infinite love, so tender, in the love manifested for us in His Son, Jesus Christ, we will humbly understand also our own individual poverty and nothingness. We will see how self-centered we tend to be and that sin comes easier to us than doing the holy will of God. We will want, therefore, to deny ourselves for love of God, renounce our own will in order to obey perfectly the will of God. We will seek to discipline ourselves in such a way that whatever we eat, drink, or do at all, we will seek to do it for the glory of God (1 Co 10:31).

THE MEANING OF ASCETICISM

The word *asceticism*—like *mysticism*—has had a history of exaggerated misunderstanding with the result that today many persons react violently against the mere mention of anything bordering on the ascetical. Such practices conjure up, usually for moderns a picture of hair-shirts, long fasts, a Jansenistic view toward human nature, especially the body. Such who practised asceticism in times past had to be sick mentally, cases of masochism. Above all, in our age of general permissiveness that allows each person to do whatver he or she wishes on the impulse of the given moment without regard to ethical principles or, above all, without consulting the higher law of love for God and neighbor, asceticism or self-discipline to attain the end of one's life would have very little meaning. For such moderns it is a rare experience that a person could love something less in order that something better might be loved more intensely. We call it simply love through self-sacrifice. Today the first word is accepted but not the second, that of sacrifice, and hence the reality of love is totally distorted into a sick, self-seeking egoism that eventually leads to all sorts of mental aberrations.

Asceticism is derived from the Greek word *askein* which means to practise or to exercise and in Attic prose refers to the exercise of the body or to the practice of an art.[2] St. Paul uses the term in the first sense when he warns the Corinthians to abstain from contact with idolators for fear of a relapse into their former pagan ways. He stresses the need for vigilance and watchfulness, for intense effort, similar to that put forth by athletes who must control their appetites if they hope to win the crown as a prize for running in the race.

> All the runners at the stadium are trying to win, but only one of them gets the prize. You must run in the same way, meaning to win. All the fighters at the games go into strict training; they do this just to win a wreath that will wither away, but we do it for a wreath that will never wither. That is how I run, intent on winning; that is how I fight, not beating the air. I treat my body hard and make it obey me, for, having been an announcer myself, I should not want to be disqualified (1 Co 9:24-27).

Paul exhorts Christians to self-denial and mortification, the subjection of the flesh with its inordinate desires, but not because these are intrinsically evil, but only insofar as they are obstacles which impede obtaining the goal desired: eternal life in God. He has a similar teaching to the Philippians: "All I can say is that I forget the past and I strain ahead for what is still to come; I am racing for the finish, for the prize to which God calls us upwards to receive in Christ Jesus" (Ph 3: 13-15).

MARTYRDOM—THE PERFECT DISCIPLINE

Can there be any true freedom as children of God, seeking always to do His holy will and not ours, without inner discipline of ourselves? Jesus insisted upon the cross of self-denial in order that we might have a part with Him (Mt 10: 38; 16:24; Mk 8:34; Lk 9: 23; 14:27). All too often, Christians may think they would like to follow Jesus Christ, but, like the rich young man in Mark's Gospel, they have too many "possessions" (Mk 10: 17-27).

St. Peter comes on quite strongly in stressing the need for asceticism in the sense of vigilance against the attacks of an enemy:

> Be sober and watch well; the devil, who is your enemy, goes about roaring like a lion, to find his prey, but you, grounded in the faith, must face him boldly (1 P 5:8).

St. Paul describes the spiritual life in terms of a struggle, a battle, a warfare engaged against spiritual forces who seek his destruction. The aim is to seek always the will of God out of loving submission to Him. But this means to enter into the lists, the arena, and stand manfully against the attacks of the evil forces.

> Draw your strength from the Lord, from that mastery which His power supplies. You must wear all the weapons in God's armor, if you would find strength to resist the cunning of the devil. It is not against flesh and blood that we enter the lists; we have to do with princedoms and powers, with those who have mastery of the world in these dark days, with malignant influences in an order higher than ours. Take up all God's armor, then, so you will be able to stand your ground when the evil times come; and be found still on your feet, when all the task is over (Ep 6:10-13).

Various names are given in the New Testament to this invisible battle. It is depicted at one time as a battle (*pali,* in Greek); a war (*polemos*); a *catharsis* or purification; an *enkratie* or attaining control over one's lower appetites; a *nekrosis,* a dying process, a mortification.

Is it any wonder that the martyr in the early centuries of Christianity became the perfect expression of faith and of love in his readiness to give the ultimate, his very own life, in witness to the centrality of Jesus Christ in his life? Was not Jesus the perfect martyr on the Cross, loving the Father and each of us unto the full sacrifice, freely given, of His own life? The sacrifice of the Christian martyr is not just the dying but the uniting of self to the Father in love. Ignatius of Antioch pleaded with the Christians in Rome to allow him to die, torn to bits by the savage beasts in the amphitheater because he wanted to be ground as wheat is ground to become one with Christ. "Now I begin to be a true disciple, through suffering and martyrdom."

Martyrdom was seen as the perfect living out of the Christian Baptism. In the immersion of the Christian into the waters of Baptism, the total man is submerged in death, symbolically, to selfish sinning in order that the same total man may put on the new life brought to us in Christ. Martyrdom is the final crown to a lifetime of such death to selfishness. It is the crown of God's love working within us to transform us into a similar love oblation to Him. This is the end and fulfillment of the Christian life.

ASCETICISM IS THE PREPARATION FOR MARTYRDOM

Asceticism is the preparation for martyrdom. Asceticism meets eventually in a heroic degree martyrdom, whether that martyrdom be an actual physical one or an interior state of continued dying to self. For both mean ultimately perfect self-surrender to God as the supreme reality in one's life. There can be no new level of awareness that God is our *all* unless there be a wrenching of ourselves out of the self-containment of a lower level. Asceticism, therefore, is more of a mental attitude that comes through an experience in prayer that God is all loving. As we learn that He alone must be adored and praised, we manfully strive to put to death all other affections and attachments to lesser loves.

In deep prayer we learn to penetrate within ourselves at levels beyond our habitual control, to enter the core of our being and there to find the spark of divine creativity which enables us to give ourselves in unselfish love to God and others. This is true liberation, a true expansion of our human consciousness as persons, freely taking our lives in hand and giving them back in love to God who has given us all in Christ Jesus. This is a resurrection to a new and higher level of life. The law of God universally operating on all levels of nature holds true also in regard to our self-development. To "ascend" to a higher form of existence, a greater liberation, we must undergo a "descending" process, a dying to the elements in our total make-up that act as obstacles to a higher mode of existence. The more we live on a purely secular level with no reflective reference to God, the less of asceticism will be in our lives. The more we give up our selfish aggrandizement by thinking in terms of others in loving service, the more we prepare ourselves for a fuller living according to our total nature as God destined us to live.

A WHITE MARTYRDOM

Death to sinful attachments and ultimately physical death in martyrdom are only the negative expression of true asceticism. The more positive aspect is that of putting on the mind of Christ, of imitating Him who alone is the way, the truth and the life (Jn 14:56). St. Paul exhorts the early Christians: "That is why I beg you to copy me, . . . he (Timothy) will remind you of the way that I live in Christ, as I teach it everywhere in all the churches" (1 Co 4:17).

Putting on the virtues that Jesus lived by in His earthly life is, therefore, a necessary part of asceticism that frees us from our sinful selves, but imitating Him becomes our most powerful motive for living as free children of God. Jesus Himself exhorted His followers: "Shoulder My yoke and learn from Me, for I am gentle and humble in heart and you will find rest for your souls" (Mt 11: 29-30).

Jesus exhorts all to put aside sinful ways, to purify the vessel from within, to turn the other cheek, to love our enemies, to do good even to those who hurt us. The epistles of the New Testament are nothing but a continued exhortation not only to avoid sin but to practise Christ-like virtues. Christianity, therefore, is a religion of our *doing*, always presupposing God's grace in moving our wills to desire to live virtuously. The Greek Fathers call asceticism *praxis*, all that man had to do in order to cooperate in his sanctification to live "according to the Image and Likeness," that is Jesus Christ.

But that cooperation necessitates a control of our appetites which tend toward immoderation. It means imposing limits according to the mind of God communicating the extent of our moderation. And this spells for all of us suffering, a going against ourselves, in a word, the Cross that Jesus Christ promised to those who would have a part with Him.

When martyrdom, the crown of a lifetime of privations and sufferings endured for the name of Jesus, was no longer the common way of dying to self since the Roman emperors had become Christians and favored Christianity as the official religion of the Roman Empire, the life of imitating Christ by a lifetime of virtues became a white-martyrdom. Virginity or continence became the most appreciated ascetical practice in imitation of Christ. Origen in the third century describes Christian asceticism as primarily a life of virginity:

> I will describe the mode of life of our ascetics. We often meet with Christians who might marry and thus spare themselves the aggravation of the struggle between the flesh and the spirit. They prefer to refrain from exercising their right, and to lay upon themselves hard penances, to subdue their bodies by fasting, to bring them under obedience by abstinence from certain foods, and thus in every way to mortify by the spirit the works of the flesh. [3]

In this interior martyrdom the Christian passes beyond the arena of comfort or convenience and begins to climb toward Calvary. There is a martyrdom endured for Christ of false accusation, of loneliness, of injustice, of ridicule, of misunderstanding, of calumny. There is a martyrdom of poverty, both actual and of the spirit, of feeling one's creatureliness in utter dependence upon God as the Giver of all good gifts. There is a martyrdom of submitting oneself to the Christian community and the authority of the spiritual leader of other leaders to interpret for the individual the mind of God. Ultimately, the interior martyrdom is one of surrendering in faith, hope and love to God in all things.

MONASTICISM

Thus the religious life evolved in the fourth century from the men and women, called the ascetics or athletes of

God, who literally went into the physical deserts of Egypt and Syria and there aggressively sought to attack and eliminate by the power of the Holy Spirit all that was of the world, the flesh and the devil in them. The darkened prisons where Christians wasted away, the amphitheaters where voracious beasts tore the martyrs apart were replaced by the immense desert. But the real desert, the amphitheater now becomes the interior depths of the individual who, in silence, wages the battle against the demonic within him. These early monks, men and women, were seeking only to live the Gospel as perfectly as they could. They were denying themselves and putting on Jesus Christ.

In the solitude of their hearts they faced themselves. They guarded their hearts; they were vigilant over each thought in order that they could bring it into a healing. In the conflict against their false selves, they cried out that Jesus would be their Lord and Savior. They were following St. Paul's exhortation to become freed of sin and become "slaves of righteousness" (Rom 6:18). They were becoming the new creation by having put to death the old man (2 Co 5:17).

The life of the monk of the desert was a revolution of his interior self.

> Your mind must be renewed by a spiritual revolution so that you can put on the new self that has been created in God's way, in the goodness and holiness of the truth (Ep 4:23-24).

He truly sought to bring every thought as prisoner, captured to be brought into obedience to Jesus Christ (2 Co 10: 5-6).

Such early ascetics understood that the ascent toward God began with a descent into themselves. They had to break through the initial fear of leaving the world of sense and psychic experiences that so easily assures most of us of our own self-sufficiency in order to descend into their true *ego* that was constantly being made according to the likeness of Jesus Christ by the power of the indwelling Holy Spirit.

The end of the ascetical life was the same for all Christians, whether they lived in a monastery or in the world. Such a distinction between those who lived the life of the evangelical counsels (read: monks, religious) and the other Christians who followed the precepts did not exist in the early Church. St. Gregory of Nyssa summarizes what all of the early Fathers taught: "There is only one vocation given to all those who believe in Him . . . that is to be called Christians."[4]

In the East, therefore, there were not two spiritualities, one monastic and one for the laity. There was only one, that which flowed from the Gospels and was summarized most perfectly in the monastic spirit. St. John Chrysostom clearly brings this out:

The Holy Scriptures do not know any such distinctions. They enjoin that all lead the life of the monks even if they are married. Listen to what Paul says (and when I say Paul, I say also Christ) in writing to married men who have children. He demands from them the same rigorous observance as that demanded from monks. He removes all luxury in their dress and food in writing: 'Women are to pray, decently attired, adorning themselves with modesty and restraint, not with braided hair, gold, pearls or expensive clothing, but with good deeds as befits women who make profession of worshipping God.' (1 Tm 2:9). And again: 'She who gives herself up to pleasure is dead while she is still alive' (1 Tm 5:6). And again: 'If then we have something with which we can nourish and clothe outselves, let us be content with it' (1 Tm 6:8). What could we demand more of from the monks?[5]

Another name for these monks who were simple men and women, not priests, truly lay-persons who were the seriously striving Christians, the ascetics, was that which they themselves coined: "Those who wish to be saved." This phrase that shows a constant preoccupation in their austere, ascetical life with final salvation occurs continually in the writings of the Fathers of the desert. In the collection of sayings from these Fathers, the famous *Apophthegmata Patrum* we read the constant introductory remark made by any disciple to his spiritual guide: "Give me some advice on how I can be saved." The spiritual elder would proceed then to tell the disciple, either a monk or a layman living in the world, it made little difference, the style of life, what are the means that all Christians must take in order to be saved.

Praying day and night and remembering the presence of God was the main ascetical preoccupation for all Christians as Jesus Himself insisted along with St. Paul (Lk 21:36; 18:1; 1 Th 5:17). This was the essence of being a *monochos*, an integrated human being, living fully according to God's purpose. The ascetic is the Christian athlete who exercises himself and tones up his body so as to be ready to give all to Christ. Origen first develops the concept of the ascetic as soldier who wages constant battle, taking prayer, penance and self-control as his weapons, a concept that gains more and more favor as the reality of martyrdom fades into the background.[6]

Gradually, however, monasticism became the place where serious Christians entered a course of ascetical practices that would allow them to be present to Christ, in the dispositions of a martyr, ready to give all if asked. Other medieval religious orders down to the modern religious congregations and even lay institutes have been modeled on the monastic ideal, " . . . if you, through the Spirit, do mortify the deeds of the body, you shall live" (Rm 8: 13(KJV). And with such a dichotomy of body and soul, the secular and the sacred worlds, there was a separation between the ascetical practices and the mystical life, the union attained with God and neighbor. Religious life could be so easily presented as a round of spiritual exercises sought to "mortify" this or that faculty, part of the human person. The wearing of the hair shirt, the use of the "discipline," as a whipping cord to bring the flesh into submission, the wearing of "chains" around the waist or legs or arms, were all ways invented by certain "ascetics" to allow the religious to bring his body and all of his appetites under submission to Christ. "Asceticism became a matter of reproducing the likeness of Christ, copying His poverty and humiliation, suffering as He did on the cross."[7]

A MORE EXCELLENT WAY

Another approach toward asceticism so prevalent in religious formation of the West has been built on the principle of *divide and conquer.* Our faults and vices were to be replaced by an array of sparkling virtues. This meant that the individual had to focus all of his intention on acquiring a certain virtue, as Archbishop Alban Goodier humorously explains in his work, *A More Excellent Way.* One week was dedicated to a given virtue which when one acquired (whatever that meant!), one pushed on to the conquest of another virtue. Records were kept of the progress made in such acts performed throughout the day according to the given virtue desired. In no time, we were supposed to be ready for canonization, for didn't the *Imitation of Christ* tell us that if we got rid of one fault and acquired one virtue each year we would soon be saints? But it really does not work that way. There must be a more excellent way still!

There is a basic principle in the spiritual life that teaches the necessity of the whole person being the subject of continuous control. We can see how perhaps we could attain some freedom from inordinate attachments and even sinful actions by a strict control over our appetites for food and sex, but, while we concentrate on these areas other vital areas of our life can be ignored and thus enslave us to inordinate or passionate immoderation unless those areas also be controlled. But that is precisely the weakness of our traditional teaching of the ascetical life.

THE ASCETICISM OF PRAYER

You can fight mosquitoes in a woods in two ways. You can wait for the pesty little creatures to attack you, one by one, or you can apply to yourself some insect repellent. The first step in freedom through asceticism must be that of prayer. Prayer is not used as an ascetical practice to wear the body down. It is a state of entering into our deeper selves, our hearts, and there to experience before the indwelling Trinity a harmony of body, soul and spirit. We experience the dignity to which God is always calling us to respond as His loving children.

In such prayer our deepest "I"—our true self—touches God and knows through His Holy Spirit who our real person is in His creative love. It is to be enlightened by grace to know our *logos,* our likeness to God's *Logos*, Jesus

Christ, in whom we find our true being. Asceticism, as a freeing action, must begin by going beyond the surface projections of our superficial self. Praying deeply allows us to become obedient to God's Spirit. "Everyone moved by the Spirit is a son of God" (Rm 8:14).

We enter into God's eternal *now* to allow Him to love us in His Word, the *Logos.* Experiencing the oneness within our being and our oneness with God, we can go out and continue to live according to the *logoi* of all things in God's *Logos.* We move away from imperatives and commands to embrace true freedom of acting according to our true potential as loving children of God. We become listeners of God's Word being spoken in each moment. Our total dignity as children of God gives us the highest motivating ideal. This is the truth according to which God has created us. When we seek to live with such motivation, true freedom results.

Our acts that flow out of our desire to love God supremely have true moral and humanizing value. Jacques Leclercq writes:

> The inner life constitutes an indispensable and essential means. In order to unify our life in God, we must direct our thinking, realize what God is, just how all value in general and in particular is related to Him. We shall never set our life in order unless we have clear and habitual consciousness, as actual as possible, of the way in which each of our acts is related to the general task of reduction to the One which we must achieve . . . Action can only be well ordered if we fix our mind on the One to start with. This is achieved in recollection only if our consciousness of the One has become sufficiently deep for us to be able to refer to it spontaneously whenever we are called to act.[8]

It is true that the inner life of prayer has a danger of making us too self-centered. But this danger dissolves if it is a matter of true prayer, or true purity of heart, of sincere listening to God speaking His word in each event. This is where true asceticism unto liberation must always begin and continue.

PURITY OF HEART

The fruit of such attentive listening to the *Logos,* the Mind of God, speaking to our individual *logos* to come and accept that invitation to live according to our full potential as children of God is what Cassian calls *purity of heart.* Purity of heart is true love. This perfect love is the love of the son who loves the Father, not out of fear, not out of hope of reward, but for love's sake alone.[9]

To know such love means to be free from all attachments.[10] Love of God is direct in that it stands under the whole created world, returning love for love in an ever humble act of homage that hands back the whole of creation to Him out of love for Him who made creation. Elizabeth Barrett Browning captures this idea beautifully in a short poem:

Earth's crammed with Heaven
and every common bush
afire with God.
And only he who sees
takes off his shoes.
The rest sit round it
and pluck blackberries.

Such purity of heart is the gaining of a true humility as

one no longer selfishly exploits creation for one's own selfish purposes. In sacrificing the splendor of creation for the sake of Him who made it, one comes to realize, in the suffering that is born in detachment of self, how great the Creator and His love must be, if one can be so attached to what is always less than He.

It is in such true love that free love is born since now it is a pure love, a love given for no other reason but for itself. Love not given freely is not truly love. Thus the true Christian life does not consist in any particular practice or following any exterior ritual, but consists primarily in the voluntary effort, willed by us, to seek in all things the Logos of God.

GUARDING THE HEART

Jesus had taught us:

> But the things that come out of the mouth come from the heart, and it is these that make a man unclean. For from the heart come evil intentions: murder, adultery, fornication, theft, perjury, slander. These are the things that make a man unclean (Mt 15:18-20).

It is the interior activity of one's mind that is all-important in prayer and in the proper use of all creatures to praise God. All external activity, unless the mind or heart accompanies it and directs it to God's praise and glory is useless before God. If our hearts, the deepest levels of consciousness, are fixed in loving adoration and obedience to God, no enemy can touch us. In fact, then the world of temptations becomes the arena where we, in conflict, can be tested and grow into a deeper, purer love for God.

To describe this attention to the presence of God,

revealing His mind to us in His *Logos* in each moment and
in each event, the early Fathers called "guarding the mind"
or "keeping the heart silent." It was to "enclose the mind
and heart," "bringing the mind under control" or "con-
taining the mind in the heart, freed of all imaginings."¹¹ It
means a loving attention and vigilance over every thought
and movement of the "heart," the deepest layers of our
consciousness and even the unconscious. It is what Teilhard
de Chardin calls "passionate indifference," the sensitive
turning to God within to see whether this or that thought is
really in harmony with the Heavenly Father's will.

The Greek Fathers summarized true Christian
asceticism leading to inner freedom by their doctrine of
nepsis. Nepsis comes from the Greek word *nepo* which
means to be sober, not inebriated or intoxicated. It refers to
a mental sobriety, a mental balance, an internal disposition
of attention to the movement of God's Spirit leading us to
true discernment of how we should react to any given
situation or temptation according to our true dignity as
God's loving children. In this state we are not moved
impulsively by our own passions, but we hold ourselves in
abeyance until we know what this or that thought is all
about in God's *Logos*. God is the living criterion of our
choices and as often as we choose according to His holy will
the freer we become as His children. Freedom, therefore, is
not primarily having the possibility of choosing good or evil,
but ultimately choosing always the good according to God's
Logos. This is true integration of ourselves according to the
likeness of God, brought about by fidelity to the interior
living Word of God within us.

KNOW THYSELF

We become the desires that we entertain. We create the world we perceive, but we perceive according to the inner thoughts, the temptations that rise up from within us, to call us into creativity according to the Word of God or into slavery as we choose solely according to our own selfish projections. Asceticism that truly frees must also be a controlled vigilance over each thought and each movement of the heart. True freedom must be won by a constant battle over the powers of darkness that lie within us, in our *heart*. It is in contrast to this darkness that God as light comes into our consciousness and tells us that the way of light is true freedom and happiness and the way of darkness is unto slavery and sickness and death. God is still telling us, His People, as He did the Israelites:

> I set before you life or death, blessing or curse. Choose life, then, so that you and your descendents may live, in the love of Yahweh your God, obeying His voice, clinging to Him; for in this your life consists, and on this depends your long stay in the land which Yahweh swore to your fathers Abraham, Isaac and Jacob He would give them (Dt 30:19-20).

The masters of Christian asceticism have drawn up the list of the eight capital temptations or sins, the roots of all sin and slavery. The first step that enslaves us and takes us away from our loving Father is the desire for some physical good: concupiscence for food or sex. The Chosen People in Egypt were faced with the great vice of gluttony. The flesh pots of Egypt typify for Origen in his commentary on the *Book of Deuteronomy* in a symbolic way man's temptation to gluttony.[1][2]

Fornication and covetousness keep man bound to material possessions. As man moves away from the bodily attachments to those of the psyche, covetousness can also be in the interior area of honors, jealousy, envy. Anger, sadness and *acedia* center in the psyche as well. *Acedia* is what we would call ennui, boredom or tepidity in the march toward perfection. One is tempted to discouragement to give up the fight, to seek worldly distractions or dissipation. In a word, *acedia* is to relinquish asceticism in the spiritual life, to give up the vigilance once maintained. Finally, vainglory and pride attack the spirit and drive out God's Spirit in our refusal to yield humbly and in truth to His guidance. We strike out in complete autonomy as though we were our own end and center of reality.

RESIST THE BEGINNINGS

Asceticism demands an attention to the dark movements within us and a vigorous resistance to them. Though we may not describe our depression born of confusion, our simple "blahs" of every day, our middle-age blues, our petty criticisms, at least internally, according to the list of approved ascetical writers of old, still the list does present us with a handy concentration on those three levels of "temptations" of body, soul and spirit relationships. The psychology of the early Fathers in regard to the development of a temptation is still solid and meaningful for all times. The first step in a temptation is the *suggestion,* presented from the dark areas of our being.[13] We are presented with a good that consists in possession of or withdrawing from what one knows to be right. The thought becomes more appealing as we *dialogue* with it. Soon we are ready and even eager to accept the suggestion. We now want it. This leads to *captivity* and finally to *passion*, a state of continued, habitual slavery to a suggestion accepted and acted upon until our free deliberation is greatly diminished.

The best resistance to such temptations is to turn within and cry out with John Cassian: "Oh, Lord, come to my assistance! Oh, Lord, make haste to help me!" The *Jesus Prayer* is the Eastern Christian's tool to disperse the demonic within him by crying out with confidence in the mercy of Jesus: "Lord, Jesus Christ, Son of God, have mercy on me, a sinner!" [14] True Christian asceticism is not only vigilance over one's thoughts but it is a prayerful surrendering to Jesus, the Savior, in deep faith, hope and love. Temptations in themselves are not evil. They can become occasions of our growing in greater love of God and in greater inner freedom as we cry out to become "unbound," from all the bonds enslaving us to ourselves, to a false reputation before others, even before God.

LISTENING TO GOD'S WORD

God cannot fill what is already filled. He cannot give Himself to us in greater, loving union unless we can empty our hearts of all submission to selfishness. But we are not static beings. We are in process of becoming our true selves as we "listen" to God breaking into our lives and speaking His Word of infinite love. God's uncreated energies pour into our daily lives, into each moment. God cannot cease to love us with an everlasting love, but that means He loves us in this concrete moment, in this human encounter with another person, with this moment of sickness, confusion, desire for success, in this moment of humiliation and failure, in this joy and in this cross.

Asceticism for modern Christians, as for Christians of

all ages, must primarily consist in a gentle spirit that listens attentively to God's Spirit revealing that God is in-breaking with His infinite love at this moment. Such a Christian practises asceticism when he or she sees that this duty, this action, this passive acceptance of what is being done and cannot be undone, is a part of God's presence. It is beyond us to seek with our puny minds what in our lives is always willed by God and what God permits to happen.[15] But asceticism demands of the Christian a faith vision that wants to see God present somehow in each moment and thus to trust and love Him in that moment, to cooperate with His loving activity and thus seek to glorify Him. A housewife is being ascetical when she sees that she is praising God more at this moment by preparing food for her hungry family than going off to a Bible meeting. A student is practising asceticism when he works in the library on a term paper, knowing that is pleasing and part of his fulfillment of that moment. A child is practising asceticism when it is time to play and he or she plays with joy. A husband could please God in no better way than to do his work with energy and joy, honestly and with love for God and man.

Thus asceticism looks to the whole man as he brings himself in this or that moment under the guiding love of God. It is his "yes" to being a child of God, made to the likeness of God Himself. He finds the moderation in all things that St. Paul preached to the Philippians: "Rejoice in the Lord always; and again I say, Rejoice. Let your *moderation* be known unto all men. The Lord is at hand" (Ph 4: 4-5; KJV).

What makes a Christian fervent and filled with the fruit of the Holy Spirit (Ga 5:22) of love, peace and joy is a sensitive waiting on the presence of the Lord to be revealed by a lively faith, hope and love in each moment. This can come about only by a vigorous asceticism of not only going out to find God in events outside of us, but of finding God also in the dark state of ourselves within us. It is to reflect on the "real" person that we are at any given moment of our history, with the moods and feelings, the state of body, soul and spirit. It is to have the courage to look at our feelings and with faith bring God into those very feelings so they will be in "moderation" and according to His holy will. It is also to be in touch with the strong points in our character, our abilities and talents, the virtues that God has given us, the many graces with the responsibility not to waste any of them but to bring forth even a hundred more.

Asceticism is a realistic view of ourselves as God sees us. It is purity of heart that sincerely wishes to have the brokenness in a given moment brought under the healing power of Jesus Savior. Most of us do not make progress in prayer, hence in our union with the mind of God, because we lack the asceticism of self-knowledge. We simply do not reflect in God's presence and in terms of the *Logos,* His Word being spoken in each moment as to who we are and what we should be. Asceticism must primarily begin with our sinfulness and the state of our "not yet." This dark side of us must be combined with the positive side, the great dignity to which God is calling us as His loving children. Only by keeping both of these polarities together can we be said to be true Christian ascetics.

For such a Christian realist there is need to make contact with the Logos of God, not only in the actual moment but also in a fixed period each day for transcendent reflection.[16] Many of us lack the concentration and living faith to discern in the rush of each moment the delicate movements of the Holy Spirit. And so we fail to size up adequately each situation and put it under the power of God's *Logos,* Jesus Christ. Yet asceticism brings us to a most important exercise that will color our daily lives if we are faithful to such introspection. In our desire to become people of God's Word, we must be able to ponder how God has spoken His Word in so many ways of each day.

REFLECTION ON GOD'S EXISTENTIAL WORD

God has spoken His Word in Holy Scripture. This constitutes the norm for our Christian life. We are in touch with the objective God who has broken into the history of the community of mankind and has lifted the cloud from His countenance. We have seen something of His glory, something of His nature and something of ourselves, the revealed knowledge of our inner dignity to be called His children. God is consistent, therefore, as He speaks that same Word in our existential lives.

I have found this following exercise most effective as a part of a very slow, disciplined process of growth in true self-knowledge and knowledge of how God's Word operates in my life. It is the basis of Christian asceticism found in all serious "ascetics." Without this reflection upon God's activity through His Word in our daily lives we will miss God as He passes by us in so many different manifestations. Through such reflection, faithfully done each day, especially in the evening, we will be healed of all inordinate sinful tendencies. We will see the need of living virtuously, not by concentrating only on one virtue at a time but on meeting Jesus Christ as a total *I* before a loving *Thou.* All other ascetical practices will then have an integrative force since they will be always serving the total person that is confronting himself before God and seeking to live according to his inner dignity.

This is the best way I know of to come into inner freedom through asceticism. If you want to grow daily in greater faith, in infused contemplation to find God in all things, you need a time for reflective looking at God in His Word. This presupposes a vivid knowledge and meditation on the Holy Scriptures. But this exercise becomes a meditation on God's Word existentially brought into reality, of one piece with His prophetic Word in Scripture, but now seen unfolding in the context of your daily life. There is a freeing knowledge that comes in knowing God was there all that day. But in such an exercise the accent is chiefly on the present, freeing power of God's Word, Jesus Christ, to heal us as we see our concrete brokenness of the present day. The events are still fresh enough to show us the facts. We cannot dispute the results. We can only cry out with true compunction, a *metanoia* that is sincere and full of urgency. We have deeply seen our sickness, our darkness and we earnestly cry out: "Lord, Jesus Christ, Son of God, have mercy on me, a sinner!" We gain the strength then to put into practice, ascetical practice, whatever is necessary with God's grace the next day.

REFLECTIVE HEALING

PREPARATION: Each evening before retiring, place yourself in the presence of God. Recall by an act of faith, adoration, hope and love that God is very present, Father, Son and Holy Spirit. In Their holy presence you are going to listen to God's many ways in which He has loved you this day in His Word and in His Spirit.

1 *THANKSGIVING:* Begin by praising and thanking God for the many gifts He has given you in this past day.

Thank Him always in detail as you sensitively recall how many wonderful ways He gave Himself to you in so many wonderful gifts. Thank Him for the great, general gifts that always are with you: the gift of life, creation, the body, soul, spirit relationships He has given you, health of body, soul and spirit, your parents, relatives, friends, your gift of faith, your vocation, the many years of persevering in that, the gifts of your fellowmen. Then in particular for the special gifts of this day beginning with the Mass and the particular gift of Jesus Christ in the Liturgy, God's greatest gift to you, the food, drink, sleep, recreation, moments of happiness, your work, and become particular as you thank Him also for having been present in the sufferings or inconveniences of that day, physical pain, misunderstandings, failures, etc. Push yourself to see Him in all things as a Giver of life.

2. *PETITION:* Ask the Holy Spirit for enlightenment to trace through this day the many ways God has spoken His existential word in continuity with His prophetic word of Scripture. "Lord, that I may see."

3. *REVIEW:* Go through the day moment by moment, event by event, person by person that passed through your day. Listen to what God was saying through each person and each event. See how you responded to His word. Give thanks where you feel you succeeded. See where you failed, hurt someone. See in contrast to God's goodness your small return especially in the areas of many omissions where you failed to respond to God's presence.

4. *HEALING SORROW:* The main emphasis should be spent here, asking God to forgive, to heal you of any failings, injuries. Ask Him to heal those whom you may have offended or hurt this day. Cry out for the healing power of the compassionate Lord Jesus: Lord Jesus Christ,

Son of God, have mercy on me, a sinner. Realize that God can heal any injury of this day in you or caused by you in another. Feel this healing power coming over you and bathing you in new strength through God's forgiving love.

5. *SURRENDER:* Abandon to the loving energies of God the forth-coming day. See briefly the day without much anxiety or planning, simply to offer it to God, begging that He will bless it, be there in each moment, helping you to live each moment dynamically in His loving presence. That day with its difficult moments, with its joys, offer it all to Him and ask that He be in each event. You wish to live tomorrow even more dynamically than today. "Take, O Lord, and receive . . ."

This daily growth in faith will bring you a progressive vision of Jesus Christ in all things and all things in Him. Virtues in the imitation of Christ will not be developed one by one but all Christian virtues will be developed together as love of Jesus Christ becomes the main focus of your attention. Duty will be replaced by the joy of being a child of God and love will be the only motivating force in your life. As Tagore writes:

I slept and dreamt that life was joy.
I awoke and saw that life was duty.
I acted and behold duty was joy!

AN ASCETICISM OF WORK

Many Christians have turned away from the necessity of asceticism in their lives chiefly because the teaching of ascetical writers in the past has all too often centered on an asceticism that was based on a separation of the sacred and the secular, the world and the Kingdom of God.

In our encounter with Christ today it is not enough to contemplate Him as the historical person revealed in the Gospels. Nor is it enough to contemplate Him in the encounter of faith through grace by which we become united with Him and the other members of His Mystical Body as branches to the vine. We must also be able to meet Christ in the divine, continual act of creation, redemption and sanctification of the total universe. His loving activity for us individually is discovered in an intuition of faith that reveals Christ as the keystone to the multiple mystery of created being. In Him we discover the *Absolute,* the beginning and the end of all unity in the cosmos. " . . . for in Him were created all things in heaven and on earth: everything visible and everything invisible . . . and things were created through Him and for Him" (Col 1:16).

Faith gives us the eyes to see, not *what* God is but, in His personal, loving activity over the millenia for us, destined children of God, *who* He is. But to foster a steady growth of faith, an environment, a *divine milieu,* to use the term of Teilhard de Chardin, must be created in which Christ can be personally contacted. He is to be found at the root, the ground of our very existence. Each moment, each atom, is to be a meeting point with the Risen Lord. Such an asceticism of purified faith brings us to a realization that the whole world is a diaphanous meeting point in which God shines forth to us.

Modern Christians cannot afford the sick luxury of retreating from the world into a piety and asceticism that refuses to consider Christ working in our work. We must develop, through faith in the Risen Lord present within the material world, a deep love of God through a passionate love of the world. A modern asceticism will insist on an ardent desire for greater self-development and the development of the whole material world that is accompanied by an inner striving for greater detachment from the things of this world.[17]

We will, therefore, find our main asceticism through our daily work because of our Christian faith that the glorious power of Christ's resurrection touches not only the soul of man but also his body and the whole sub-human cosmos to "confer the hope of resurrection upon their bodies."[18] This is the vision that St. Paul had of man in his most creative, free act becoming with Jesus Christ a co-creator, a co-operator, a "reconciler" of the whole world back to the Father (2 Co 5:19).

But what a deep asceticism is needed to prevent power that derives from the use of our creativity from making us into little gods! Interior detachment in all of our activities and also in the passive diminishments that come to us in the process of living dynamically in cooperation with God's creative activities is demanded at each moment. Development of our powers and those of the universe and renunciation are not to be opposed as found in an earlier form of Christian asceticism. Attachment and detachment are necessary complements. The cross and resurrection are two phases of the seed maturing into the fruit. Matter and spirit, body and soul, evil and good, are all interrelated phases of a continuous progression in true, ontological life, the life that Christ came to give us in greater abundance. The unifying element is precisely our faith that God in His immanence is in all His creatures, acting to fulfill them because He looks on them and sees them as good (Gn 1:25).

ASCETICISM LEADS TO CONTEMPLATION

Through such asceticism of work done for the glory of God to fulfill the world the Christian is led progressively to greater inner freedom. He moves away from his distorted way of interpreting events and persons encountered through his own insecurities and aggressive attacks. He finds that each event is an encounter with the *Logos,* the Lord Jesus Christ Himself, in and through the very material creatures. He it is who gives reality to each being. He it is who evolves the whole universe into the "new creation" foretold by St. Paul (2 Co 5:17-19). In such an atmosphere of faithful contemplation of the Logos in all things, we can respond in full freedom to give ourselves in a return of love to Him. This is the final stage of true freedom: the freedom that love of God and neighbor begets within us. It is a freeing of our false selves so as to live dynamically according to the full potential within us. This is the aim of true asceticism that leads always, if it is authentic, to deeper union in love with God and the whole universe. Let us see how true freedom, therefore, is really love.

8

The Freeing Power of Love

The most heart-gnawing experience that we can know is that of loneliness. God has made us for love, to love and to be loved. He who is Love [1 Jn 4:8] has implanted deep within all of us these burning desires to leave our isolated selves and stretch out with the fullness of our being to say "yes" to another. Distances and the barriers of body and soul through sin can keep us isolated from our deeper self. We withdraw from loving encounters, afraid to reach out toward new life, new richness through love.

Have you ever been alone with yourself, away from crowds and distractions, and felt in that moment both a disgust for how unfilfilled you were as a human being and yet a craving to come alive before it was too late? I guess that is where death has its greatest sting. We know we were made for so much more. Now it looks as though our opportunities for growth in this life are closing in upon us.

In such moments of "ultimate concern," to use Paul Tillich's phrase, we have a breakthrough in knowledge. The monolithic person we thought we were yields to all sorts of persons, all within us, living and asserting themselves with varying degrees of dominance. We are aware of the self that we see in the mirror, that others see and call by our name. This is Carl Jung's *persona*, fashioned mainly by our sense experiences from the world immediately around us. It is an important part of us. This person has inherited many characteristics from our parents. He has been fashioned in a certain way by education. Social environment has molded him according to certain habits of acting and thinking. Persons have loved us and allowed us to love them in differing degrees of intimacy. Others have put us down. We were scarred by their lack of love. We closed up against them and this became an habitual way of acting before the unknown and suspected in our lives.

There is also another person within me, the person I would like to be. Perhaps I am constantly striving to be that person. But this, too, is not my freest self, because I often disregard the former person with all of his experiences and I live according to a projected image that I believe myself to be.

THE INNERMOST SELF

Yet deep within us echoes another *self*. Down through all the levels of our life-experiences and idealistic desiring there is the haunting voice of a person that we seem to know vaguely. That person is bathed in light, peace and joy. He calls us to leave the binding slavery of the other levels and to enter into true freedom. It is the true self that God indwells, our being as spirit capable of communicating freely and spontaneously with God's Spirit.

Living on this level is like rising from a sickbed to step out into the brightness of a fresh, spring day and begin to live fully an exhilarating liberation. No longer do we have to obey our nagging selves, slaves to opinions of others as the sole criterion of truth, slaves to our own distorted image, our habitually low profile of ourselves or victimized by an ideal that is equally unreal. Above all, we now are called to deeper interiority, no longer guided by narcissism. There is now a new-gounded sense of honesty, of wholeness and courage to accept the truth that now seems to flow in a free communication at each moment as we listen to the Voice deep within us.

It is, in the words of Shakespeare: "To thine own self be true." Soren Kierkegaard describes it as: "To be that self which one truly is."[1] We have already called it according to the scriptural term, "living in the heart." This is a movement towards freedom and this is always an exciting, yet harrowing experience. Freedom is a move toward self-determination, ultimately towards a loving gift of self to another, and this necessitates a real *dying* process. It is moving away from values that were extrinsic to us and yet those values determined our choices.

Dr. Carl Rogers describes this freedom:

> Freedom to be oneself is a frighteningly responsible freedom, and an individual moves toward it cautiously, fearfully, and with almost no confidence at first . . . They are in flux, and seem more content to continue in this flowing current.[2]

Such a person is daily making contact with his "innermost" self. He listens to his inner feelings, seeking to become more alive, more aware of life within at a deeper level of awareness than that lived before. At the same time he lives with greater sensitivity towards others, seeing into their "innermost" self beyond the superficial impressions first received.

HEART SPEAKS TO HEART

As we learn to live interiorly, our progress is a movement away from our masculine dominated, rationally controlled self to a more intuitive grasp of reality. A new knowledge is given. At first is is experienced as coming out of our deep reservoir where it seemingly always existed, yet unknown to our superficial self. Its depths seem to stretch downward into infinity. Gradually as we have courage and sincerity to surrender to this new knowledge, we become aware that it flows from a communicating Person, indwelling within us. He becomes gradually more present to us. We learn to let go and surrender to His loving presence. We experience an integrating process taking place between the feminine and masculine aspect within us. We are becoming an *I,* now in free, loving dialogue with God as a *Thou,* an indwelling presence.

We sense Aristophanes' explanation in Plato's *Symposium* to be a true picture of ourselves. In the beginning of time all of us were not divided into male or female. We did not have one head, two arms, etc. but we were double everything, put together back to back, yet still only one person. We were all split into two parts and the parts separated. Integration takes place at this deep level and it takes place most perfectly in that state of being that we call *contemplation.*

This is more than praying, above all, saying prayers. It passes beyond even words and images that we entertain of ourselves and of God.

Contemplation is basically a look turned toward God. It is a human being standing, as it were, outside of the habitual ideas that he has of himself, the person that he thinks he is. It is his getting down below that false everyday ego and getting into his deepest source where he stands before God, consciously turning toward his Source, his Origin. . . . It does not consist in having beautiful thoughts, nor in having any emotions, sentiments, or piety. It consists fundamentally in standing before God, not with one faculty perceiving some facet of God but with man's total being absorbed into the total being of God. It is the return of my whole being back to God as a gift that expresses the attitude which I call worship-prayer, the ultimate point of contemplation.[3]

But to reach this state of *being in* God, communicating with Him, not in words or images, but in the silence of a *yes* continually spoken in oblational love, requires a long process of dying to self. And we are so reluctant to agree to die!

PERFECT LOVE

In Iris Murdoch's novel, *The Unicorn,* we have a description of a man who, faced with imminent death reaches a moment of "perfect" love. Effingham Cooper, a very self-centered person never having known true love, finds himself trapped in a bog. As he is being sucked down deeper and deeper into the mud, after the initial panic, he collects himself. His egotistic life passes before him and in the darkness of imminent death, he sees a beautiful, streaming light. He has a flash of intuition as to what true love is.

Since he was mortal he was nothing, and since he was nothing all that was not himself was filled to the brim with being, and it was from this that the light streamed. This then was love which was the same as death. He looked and knew, with a clarity which was one with the increasing light, that with the death of the self the world becomes quite automatically the object of a perfect love. He clung to the words "quite automatically" and murmured them to himself as a charm.[4]

For Murdoch, love is an awareness that other persons and things exist with an independence from ourselves. We do not create the world. God does. And He creates each creature with a particularity and uniqueness that depends solely upon God's personal love for that creature. Contemplation is a dying to our own control over reality to become vulnerable to the uniqueness of the other. Love is the movement made possible in contemplation towards the sacredness in the other person. It follows fast upon the prior movement of humility, a chastening and purification of our own powerized view of persons and things as though they belonged to us!

The self, as center of the entire world around which all things move in orbit and in dependence, caves in. The illusion of such unreality yields to a new insight. The otherness of others not only makes me different from them but I am now in a position to love them. Love is possible only when there are two centers of independence and uniqueness ready freely to take their individual center and unite it with the other center. By recognizing the difference and uniqueness of each person can we begin to be excited about an enriching union in freedom. It is what Martin Buber called the *I-Thou* experience as over an *I-It* relationship.

James Baldwin poignantly characterizes the separation of black people from "others" in his *The Fire Next Time,* but such a feeling of estrangement is more universally felt than merely along lines of color.

Yes, it does indeed mean something—something unspeakable—to be born, in a white country, an Anglo-Teutonic, anti-sexual country, black. You very soon,

without knowing it, give up all hope of communion. Black
people, mainly, look down or look up but do not look at
each other, not at you, and white people, mainly, look away
. . . The universe which is not merely the stars and the
moon and the planets, flowers, grass and trees, but *other
people,* has evolved no terms for your existence, has made
no room for you, and if love will not swing wide the gates no
other power will or can.[5]

GOD'S LOVE, ETERNALLY PERFECT

Perhaps and hopefully, all of us have been caught up
in deep prayer or in deep, loving communication with
husband, wife, friend, man or woman or God. In a flash,
barriers seemed non-existent. Love swung wide the gates
and there we were. Two persons in one. We knew each
other beyond time. Something in the other said there was a
need and something in me cared with tenderness and gave.
There was no need for reason, yet it all had a wonderful,
wordless reason. If we experience oneness with a beloved
friend, how much deeper ought such oneness be experienced in our loving union with God?

We have seen the freedom of God, both in the loving
union of Father and Son in their Spirit and in the Trinity's
free love for us as individuals. We can, at rare moments,
take wing and fly up and beyond our habitual level of
consciousness. Like an eagle with mighty pinions, we hover
over the world, one with all, all in one. Yet within the
Trinity there is perfect recognition of the uniqueness and
reverence for the Other. There is a *caring* to serve the
Other, to gift the Other totally with Self-Gift. And thus
there is perfect and total giving and perfect and total
possessing of the Other.

This is what *indwelling* means. Each dwells in the Other. Each is totally present as Gift and Receiver to the Other, Father and Son by means of the unifying force of the Spirit who alone can preserve uniqueness of independence along with dependent need of oneness with each other.

The following poem hopefully conveys something of this indwelling of the Father and the Son:

NEAREST THE HEART OF THE FATHER

The Son is nearest
the heart of the Father.
"In sinu Patris."
He "insinuates" Himself,
enters into the Heart
of His Father.
They embrace,
surround each other
like a mother covering her baby,
like two lovers made one
in exstatic embrace.
O God, cover me.
Embrace me!
Make me one
as You and Jesus are one.
Draw me into Your Heart.
Immerse me deeply into Yourself.
If human love can heal
all division and separation;
if lovers know only oneness,
what must it be
to be nearest
the Heart of the Father,
"in sinu Patris"?[6]

GOD'S FREE LOVE FOR US

One of the most thought-provoking murals that I have ever seen, done by the artist, Michael Dvortsak, dominates the wall behind the altar in the Newman Chapel of the University of California at Santa Barbara in Goleta, California. Jesus Christ is vaguely outlined as the suffering Savior on the Cross. The vivid symbols of a living world tumble forth from His left hand and fall down in a circular movement that catches, as in a mightly flood of love, the whole created world of inner space of sub-microscopic life as well as that of outer space, of the macrocosm, of planets, galaxies and quasars.

The artist has given to the face of Christ not only one of suffering but a look of intense interest and spiritual concern towards every created atom. From St. Paul's vision: " . . . for in Him were created all things in heaven and on earth, everything visible and everything invisible" (Col 1:16), the artist shows how all of creation, from the individual unicell of life, to the union of sperm and ovum, to the formation of the foetus, comes from Christ, through Him and in Him. From the mountains and valleys making up man's complicated inner, physical world, to the planets and galaxies of outer space, all things sweep out and down in the shape of a human heart from the head of Christ, back up from the bottom through the figure of Christ.

We see in this painting a portrayal of God's creative love. The world pulsates in each atom with God's loving, uncreated energies. God loves the created world through Christ in His Spirit. The Spirit is the sweeping force of love that fashions the Body of Christ, the Son of God into a unity. "There is one Body, one Spirit, just as you were all called into one and the same hope when you were called" (Ep 4:4).

The Body of Christ is being fashioned by the material "particulars" of this universe, as each atom is brought by man, the contemplator, under the power of Christ. God loves the world that is of His making. He looks upon it in all its uniqueness and singularity in each individual creature and loves it as good (Gn 1:10).

Yet God in Christ looks down from the Cross and suffers. The world groans in travail. God in Christ lives and dies in order that through His Love, the Spirit, He might bring all into His love. The artist is saying that there is hope for our material world. There is an ordering force inside of the material world giving it direction, drawing all diversity into a oneness by God's infinite love.

THEOSIS—THE GOAL OF GOD'S LOVE

God is gentle and patient, signs of His deep love for us. He is not far removed from the monotony, the slow growth, even the set-backs, the pains and the sufferings. He is, indeed, "inside," present in His loving activities, seeking only to share Himself more and more completely since that is the nature of free love. It is not primarily to receive that one, especially God, loves another. God loves us not because of what we can give Him but because He is so overflowing with exuberant richness that He wishes to share His very richness, His very self, with us.

G.K. Chesterton gives us one of my favorite passages in his work *Orthodoxy:*

A child kicks his legs rhythmically through excess, not absence, of life. Because children have abounding vitality, because they are in spirit fierce and free, therefore they want things repeated and unchanged. They always say, 'Do it again;' and the grown-up person does it again until he is nearly dead. For grown-up people are not strong enough to exult in monotony. But perhaps God is strong enough to exult in monotony. It is possible that God says every morning, 'Do it again' to the sun; and every evening, 'Do it again' to the moon.[7]

God creates the whole world of so much exuberant richness only for us human beings. He wishes to be present to us, communicating His infinite love for us in each created gift. Yet all such gifts are ways of bringing us to that state of children of God when we finally recognize Him as our loving Father and that He loves us infinitely in our likeness to Him, that we receive Himself, as indwelling Gift, totally present to us as His love in His Spirit transforms us into a new creation.

> But to all who did accept Him
> He gave power to become children of God,
> to all who believe in the name of Him
> who was born not out of human stock
> or urge of the flesh
> or will of man
> but of God Himself (Jn 1:12-13).

Jesus promised that not only both He and the Father would indwell us but that also He would send us the Holy Spirit of union between the Father and the Son who would dwell also within us as in a temple (1 Co 3:16; 1 Co 6:19). How consoling are the words of Jesus to each of us: ". . . and my Father will love Him, and we shall come to Him and make our home with Him" (Jn 14:23).

This is the goal of our lives, the meaning of why God loves us. It is to make us His children (1 Jn 3:1-3). The

Father wishes to give Himself to each of us as He perfectly gives Himself to His Son through His Holy Spirit. He makes us independent, uniquely ourselves, free to return His love. He makes us according to the likeness of His Son and He loves us with that same *need* that He has for His Son. He is pleased when the Son returns His perfect love. He is pleased in His only begotten Son when we freely consent to love Him in Jesus.

Yet every love is built on suffering, a readiness, by being vulnerable, by caring much, to lose oneself in wanting the other. God suffers a painful love in His Son who, as man, can offer in human form a divine, perfect, free love of God Himself for each of us individually.[8] The suffering Son is present to the Father and the Spirit. If the Son suffers and is pained, the Father and the Spirit, totally present and caring for the Son, take on also His sufferings and pains.

FOR ME HE DIES

When we consider this perfect love of God indwelling us, we see how unfree we are to respond to that infinite love. No doubt we need, as was pointed out in the preceding chapter, a vigilance over the movements of the dark areas within us that prevent our true, innermost self from coming forth in response to such love offered. But we need a deeper growth in knowledge, given by God's Spirit, of our true self in Jesus Christ.

This is the person we truly are in God's eyes. It is a constant process of greater awareness of this indwelling love of God for us in our particularity. it is the Spirit of Jesus sent into our hearts that reveals the depths of God's love for us (Rm 5:5). St. Paul understood that God's infinite, perfect, present and caring love for Himself was made manifested in Christ Jesus. He is the perfect image of the Father (Col 1:15). Seeing His love for us, we see the love of the Father for us (Jn 14:9; 15:9). And so St. Paul, overwhelmed by God's love in His Word, could only mutter in amazement:

> . . . and I live now not with my own life but with the life of Christ who lives in me. The life I now live in this body I live in faith: faith in the Son of God who loved me and who sacrificed Himself for my sake (Ga 2:19-20).

GOD'S BY GRACE

There is a constant, theological and liturgical tradition among the Eastern Fathers that describes this indwelling of the Trinity within us human beings in rather strong language that would rule out any language implying a moral union. As Jesus Christ, the Incarnate Word, was full divinity and full humanity, joined together in the hypostatic union without confusion or separation so we human beings are made sons of God by grace, bringing together our humanity with God's indwelling divinity, without confusion or separation. St. Cyril of Alexandria well summarizes the Greek patristic common teaching on divinization:

> For He alone is both the Only-begotten and the First-born; Only-begotten as God; First-born insofar as He became through the salvific union a man among us and among many brothers. By this we also in Him and through Him according to nature and grace have been made sons of God. According to nature insofar as we are one in Him (through the same human nature); by participation and according to grace through Himself in the Spirit.[9]

It is the work of the Holy Spirit to deify our human nature, first in Baptism when we become through the Holy Spirit temples of God, and the work of sanctification is begun anew. Holy Eucharist, the flesh of Christ deified through union with the Divine Word, becomes the instrument of divinization of our flesh.[10]

The indwelling presence of the Trinity as an interior illumination, a light within man that permeates his whole being, integrates the body, soul and spirit levels into a "whole" human being, consumed by love for God. One walks out into this world seeing God's light everywhere, His loving presence, His harmony, His *Logos* in whom all things are created, and he adores Him in great humility. He surrenders himself in total service. He is guided by the Holy Spirit at each moment in the things of God. He knows at each moment what is the will of God for him. He sees what a child of God must do and can do with the inner, divinizing force of the indwelling Trinity drawing him to such ontological dignity and nobility.

As one continues to grow in compunction and humility, he advances in seeing the light of God's loving presence in all things. This is true contemplation which admits of a great growth in the inner knowledge of the mysteries of God. Such a spirit of continued contemplation allows the human intelligence to remain completely simple, totally integrated into God, stripped of all thoughts and bathed in the light of God. St. Symeon the New Theologian describes this state of contemplation:

> The intelligence cannot find any other object but the light on which it has been fixed . . . It rests then in the abyss of the divine light which allows it to perceive nothing outside of itself. Indeed, this is what is meant: 'God is light' and the

supreme light. For those who reach this, it is the repose of all contemplation.[11]

GOD IN MATTER

But how do we move to such a level of consciousness so that we, through contemplation, can see with our spiritual eyes God everywhere? How we long for such truth, such a grasp of reality as God sees it. How can we be freed from our darkness and world of illusions?

God in the Old and New Testaments constantly meets His children in the context of their material lives. God is present everywhere, yet as man gets in touch with himself, with his different levels of being, he is able to receive more of God's loving gift of Himself. Man is able to surrender himself more and more to God's service.

One reason why Western man has not enjoyed a progressive liberation unto greater love for God and neighbor is that he tends to remain abstract, in rational control of an inner world, but one that he is in charge of. He is the god (with small *g*) of this world as he manipulates, judges and interprets according to his own, often self-centered, needs. He is not in touch with his deeper levels of personhood because he has ignored the "situated" person that he is in the material context of his life. Through a Cartesian dichotomy between the material world and that of thought, between his body and mind, he all too often ignores the material world around, beginning with his own physical body.

In order that man can become integrated and touch his deeper self, he needs to "find" himself from the outside. How few of us truly can be at home with our physical bodies? Our competitive society, dominated by puritanical notions of good and evil and by the compulsion always to be up and doing according to the pre-conceived self-image imposed by bourgeois society, does not allow us to be quiet and, like children, to sense deeply the present moment and real self made aware of itself by profound sense impressions of the immediate world around it. Children have that wonderful sense of excitement as they are vitally in touch with the world around through strong, spontaneous sense experiences that they have not yet learned to filter out or interpret through a jaded *deja vu* attitude that we call usually among adults just simply boredom.

In order to move to new levels of awareness, we must work through our sense experiences. We must "re-learn" how to see the material world and how to experience all the uniqueness of each creature in its particularity. We need to learn how to "contemplate" the separateness of each individual thing before we can learn to care for that individual creature. Christianity, especially in its uses of strong sense experiences in the sacraments, sacramentals and above all the Divine Liturgy, has always maintained an incarnational approach to God and neighbor through the material world of strong, vivid sense impressions.

But, alas, one of the great dangers of our modern life is that we have allowed our senses to atrophy through our thermostated, controlled life. Many of us are like bees, busily buzzing inside the bee-hive, but never leaving the hive to make contact with the material world of flowers which is the first step to bring forth honey. Stop sometime to allow yourself the leisure of listening to the voice of the sea, the sound of stars up in the sky at night, the laughter in the voice of a loved one. When was the last time we took a walk in the rain and felt a part of the world that was being cleansed together? Do you allow the touch of a friend to touch you and speak a language that goes beyond concepts?

In a word, I guess what I am trying to say is that because we do not live intensely sensory experiences, we are no longer "open" to move from the material world to values of a more transcendental nature. We close ourselves off from the possibility of God and our neighbor communicating to us through the material world. We have a great need today to re-educate our senses in order that they bring to consciousness sharp, vital, full sense experiences, the only way in which the material world can make contact with our interior selves, in which eventually the transcendent God can become truly the core of our immanent true selves.

If we are to learn how to live in touch with our deeper, true selves, to be motivated by love and self-sacrifice towards God and neighbor, to be, in a word, contemplatives, we need to begin with a gentle receptivity towards God's created world around us. There is so much beauty if we could only be silent and listen to it shout out God's grandeur. Gerard Manley Hopkins knew how to look inside the material world and find the "inscape" in each created thing that led him to adoring love of God at the heart of matter. He wrote:

> All things are charged with love, are charged with God, and if we know how to touch them, give off sparks and take fire, yield drops and flow, ring and tell of Him.

We listen to God's *Logos* in each creature communicating God's tremendous love-presence. We cannot always find the perfect world of unspoilt nature that shouts so powerfully to us of God's presence. The secret of freeing love through contemplation is to find in the very activities of our commonplace life, in the sense experiences that are overly familiar to us from a lifetime of routine, in the loved ones we take so for granted because we have typed them into unchanging strait-jackets of our own making, that opening to God's self-giving to us in the particularity of each being as God's gift to us.

GOD'S PRESENCE IN HUMAN LOVE

As we move into our deeper self, we find the material world becoming a mirror in which we see the loving face of God. This becomes intense experiences of God's incarnational presence in our human friendships. We learn to let go of our control over others. As we learn to love in greater consciousness of God's indwelling presence at the center of our being, we progressively learn how to let His presence shine forth from the center of our loved ones' being. To the degree that I can let God be present and loving me at the center of my *I*, to that degree I can allow God to lead me to the center of my friend's true being. Gradually we see in true human love that our attitudes to our loved ones change. Even our attitudes toward God and prayer change. Prayer becomes a yielding to God's love, found everywhere. It becomes a consciousness of the intense love He has for us. It becomes a peaceful, joyful urge to surrender to His presence to serve Him in each human encounter.

Gone are the forceful, nervous attacks with their secured defenses that highlighted so many past human communication. Gentleness and patience and a joyful expectancy characterize now our meeting of others. A whole inner world that once was closed now opens up as we learn to listen to other persons. Each person is seen in his or her individuality. We respect his or her uniqueness. We strain forward to see ways of serving that inner beauty and dignity that are locked inside each person.

We strive to see the *Logos* of Jesus Christ loving in His Spirit the *logos* of that person. A new power, the love of Jesus Christ, has become a living force operating from deep within our hearts. "The inner man is renewed day by day" (2 Co 4:16). "And this is because the love of Christ overwhelms us . . . " (2 Co 5:14). The closer we touch God living and loving within us ourselves and His whole world of other human persons redeemed by the blood of Jesus Christ, the closer we touch others also in the depths of their beings. God's love strengthens us to love others. In loving others with God's very own love within us, we grow in greater love of God.

> If we love one another, God dwells in us and His love is perfected in us . . . and we have known and believed the love that God has for us. God is love; and he that dwells in love dwells in God and God in him (1 Jn 4:12, 16).

Moments spent with loving friends become moments of contemplating God's beauty in delicate, sensitized communion with the ones we love. In such love we are humbled that God and friend have opened their beings to us. We are privileged to enter deeply into their inner depths, into their "heart." They share their thoughts, fears, joys and desires. We accept them in their sacred revelation of themselves to us. Only responsible love in return is our answer to their offer of themselves in all their vulnerability. They have opened up areas unknown, perhaps even to themselves. We surrender all power to exploit or manipulate them.

LOVE IS CARING

When a mother gives birth to her babe, God pours into her that instinctual love that is called *caring*. It is expressed in her tireless gaze, the laughter of her eyes as she bounces the baby in her arms, in her warm, tender, surrounding embrace that somehow seems to stretch out infinitely to embrace all other babies, all other human beings, all creatures that breathe and have being in God. Jesus had this love for Lazarus as he cared for him, wept at his grave, stretched out to call him into life again. Jesus *cared* for his fellow Jews as He wept before His Father's face on their behalf. His caring love stretched out to give Himself to each person that came to Him in any state of brokenness. He healed them by His caring love.

And when His fellow countrymen rejected Him, He cared enough to weep for them and ask the Father to forgive them.

Jerusalem, Jerusalem, you that kill the prophets and stone those who are sent to you! How often have I longed to gather your children, as a hen gathers her chicks under wings, and you refused! (Mt 23:37).

Father, forgive them; they do not know what they are doing (Lk 23:34). Care is the whole person stretching out to cover, protect, warm, bring into existence the other, not merely on one level of existence but also on the deepest sharing of life's beauty and happiness. *Care* highlights the strange paradox that Jesus taught. It is only in losing our lives that we gain them in a new way (Lk 17:33). When we show loving care for another human being, God's love in us is released and actuated. We grow along with God's love as

we, whether knowingly in union with God or not, un-
selfishly love another.

When we turn away in isolated un-caring for our
brothers or sisters, we turn towards darkness and
nonentity. Hell is the state of non-identity of no true *I* in
relation to a *Thou*. Rollo May expresses this fundamental
truth of human existence:

> When we do not care, we lose our being; and care is the way
> back to being. If I care about being, I will shepherd it with
> some attention paid to its welfare, whereas if I do not care,
> my being disintegrates. [1] [2]

LOVE IS FREEING

The more we learn to care, not only for those who care
for us, but for all other human persons whom we encounter, the greater is our own personal growth in inner
freedom. We are freed of all obstacles that keep us in
unconcerned indifference towards others. We become freed
also from a selfish "using" of one in order to escape
aloneness, only to fall into an egoism *a deux,* two islands
together attacking the world.

We know from experience that our true self is con-
stituted by a greater and greater generosity in giving of
ourselves to others. We know, as a total knowledge that
touches our total state of being a human person, that we
really are a part of every other person.

Such a Christian learns to live according to St. Paul's
teaching:

> There must be no competition among you, no conceit; but
> everybody is to be self-effacing. Always consider the other
> person to be better than yourself, so that nobody thinks of

his own interests first but everybody thinks of other people's interests instead (Ph 2:3-4).

He seeks always, not for his own advantage, but for that of the other man (1 Co. 10:24).

To act in such a "self-effacing" way in order to find the image of our true self is utter nonsense if we seek to accomplish such action by our own powers. As we confess constantly before the Lord our fear of selfishness, gnawing away at our insides, God fills our emptiness with faith. Faith is not an intellectual assent to a revealed truth so much as my believing in God's revealed Word in a direct communication in prayer that God loves me. Faith is believing that others are loved also by God. It is to "see" their inner beauty that hides itself under the distracting appearances of the "outer" person. It is faith to believe that God needs me to become present to others by His love and mine together loving my neighbor. Faith leads us to trust in the next moment that there will not be this present meaninglessness. Rather, as I open myself in gift to the next moment, I hope that I shall creatively find meaningfulness in that coming event. Thus rooted in faith and hope, love as a gift from God empowers me to wait expectantly. True love loses all power but gains the only true power that exists in heaven and on earth. That power is the weakness of God to give Himself to inferior man. Yet, in that gift of Himself in His Word, God rejoices in new relationships as He experiences His holiness and goodness. He rejoices as man returns His love and allows God to be loved. Not even God can give Himself the joy of being beloved by another. He, who is full of all riches, waits to become enriched by our love. He who is perfectly at rest rejoices in the dancing and feasting because His son has come home.

T.S. Eliot in *East Coker* well expresses the paradox of love and waiting in hope:

I said to my soul, be still, and wait without hope
For hope would be hope for the wrong thing; wait without love
For love would be love for the wrong thing; there is yet faith
But the faith and the love and the hope are all in the waiting,
Wait without thought, for you are not ready for thought:
So the darkness shall be light, and the stillness the dancing.[13]

LOVE AS PERSONAL GROWTH

Love admits of many expressions and an infinity of degrees of expanded consciousness of union with the one loved. But its essence consists of a movement from isolation toward a community of persons. From "Me" I move to "*We.*" It is a return to the Garden of Eden when man first came out of the creative act of the *We* in God. "Let us make man in our own image, in the likeness of ourselves" (Gn 1:26).

We are conceived in the wombs of our mother through a "We" community of husband and wife. What a powerful beginning in physical and psychic healthiness if such conception is a result of the love of two persons truly surrendering themselves to each other! How many human beings suffer their whole life long because their parents were not lovers who passed beyond the limits of selfish isolation. The child all too often was the result of egoism.

Thus many psychologists see our first "I" consciousness as rooted in the "We" of a community that not only relates us to our parents and all of their relatives but through them we are related to the "We" of the whole human race. Baptism on a spiritual level through God's Holy Spirit gives us a pre-natal sense of our true "I" in a "We" community of the Trinity but also in the "We" community of all human beings as brothers and sisters of each other in Christ Jesus under one loving Father of us all.

As we move toward the other or others in ever increasing selfless love, the *agape* of God towards us, we undergo deeper levels of expanded consciousness of our unique particularity Every time we are privileged to die to self and rise to the transcendent true self that is found only in gift of self to another, we experience a fuller freedom of an "I" toward others.

Yet, each moment of "passing over" into the darkness of mystery and the unknown, we also experience a new-founded union with the other and hence with the whole world. Each "indwelling" in the other by being more present in a loving way brings us into a oneness with the particularity or uniqueness of the other and a growing awareness that we are more and more really one with the particularity of God and each human being in world history, even one with all of creation.

For this reason, Teilhard de Chardin could describe the action of love: "Love differentiates as it unites." In his *The Divine Milieu* he writes of the *personal* in the other and yet all are to be brought into a unity in God:

. . . since my heart cannot reach Your person except at the depths of all that is most individually and concretely personal in every 'other,' it is to the 'other' himself, and not to some vague entity around him, that my charity is addressed . . . You merely, through Your revelation and Your grace, force what is most human in me to become conscious of itself at last. Humanity was sleeping—it is still sleeping—

imprisoned in the narrow joys of its little closed loves. A tremendous spiritual power is slumbering in the depths of our multitude which will manifest itself only when we have learnt to break down the barriers of our egoisms and, by a fundamental recasting of our outlook, raise ourselves up to the habitual and practical vision of universal realities.[14]

THE CHURCH OF THE FREED

When we change our perception of reality and we begin to see the world in God's *Logos,* Jesus Christ, then He becomes the beginning and the end, the Alpha and the Omega (Rv 1:8). We begin to live in the vision of the centrality of God's Word in all creatures and we work consciously to reconcile the whole universe to the Father through His Son.

> . . . so that He should be first in every way;
> because God wanted all perfection
> to be found in Him
> and all things to be reconciled through Him and for Him,
> everything in heaven and everything on earth,
> when He made peace
> by His death on the cross (Col 1:18-20).

We live in the knowledge of "the mystery of His purpose, the hidden plan He so kindly made in Christ from the beginning . . . that He would bring everything together under Christ, as head, everything in the heavens and everything on earth" (Ep 1:9-10). By living in the love of the Spirit of Jesus, we aid in building up the Body of Christ, the Church. By living freely as children of God, turning away from all selfishness, we direct the world consciously to its center, Jesus Christ. Through this body of christified persons, Christ reaches the rest of mankind and the entire material universe. Each perfection contributed to make this world a better world in which to live, no matter how banal be that action, builds up Christ's Body. The christic energy of grace deepens the reflective consciousness of the individual members and draws the individuated persons into a convergence, a union of love of each towards Christ and towards one another. Love is the "within" of things, the immanent force unifying all conscious beings, "personalizing" by totalizing.

St. Paul writes that: "If we live by the truth and in love, we shall grow in all ways into Christ, who is the head . . . " (Ep 4:15). This is the freedom that comes to us human beings from the Spirit who frees us from isolation and brings us into a loving oneness in the Body of Christ (Ep 4:4). All such growth in love of Christ comes from, through and with Him. Yet each member of His Body, the Church that we are, must continue to open up to that presence of Jesus within himself and to Jesus present outside him, in the lives of all men, guiding the whole world into the final completion. Jesus is present in His members as His whole Body grows in and through the material created world of God.

AND THE TRUTH WILL MAKE YOU FREE

So much has been written about freedom. So much more will be written in the years to come as we human beings strive to live by a greater freedom to be our true selves against a society that de-personalizes us. But these pages have been written to show that freedom is a gift from God. Man must cooperate in a conversion, a humble desire to return to the freedom of the Father's house, to "indwell" again in His loving presence and to serve Him solely out of the sheer joy of being His child. Yet even in this desire to go home and be with the Father we must see the gift of God's loving energies stirring us at the deepest level of our beings to want to become our true selves as God has wanted us to be. This is true contemplation. It is never given in one static moment. It is a process that begins in this life, continues each moment of our earthly life and accompanies us into the life to come as a continued growth in our uniqueness as persons freely loved by God in Christ Jesus along with a continued growth in the union of God and all other human beings into the very Body of Jesus Christ, His Church.

Freedom is, then, actually the love of God working within us to impower us with a self-sacrificing love toward all creatures. We become liberated as we exist on ever new levels of consciousness of this oneness with all in Christ. Freedom creates in us joy and the exciting desire to become ever more and more the whole universe as we experience a new capacity of *being* toward others and a new capacity to receive *being* from their love returned. Ultimately Heaven or the Kingdom of God is that state of inner freedom where we allow the freedom of God's love to recreate us ever anew as His children and to send us out to love one another in His love.

St. Paul assures us that "love does not come to an end" (1 Co 13:8). We can conclude this book with the thought that freedom also never comes to an end. Freedom begets more freedom just as love begets more love. The Kingdom of God that is made up of God and His freed children can best be described in the vision of St. John the Beloved Disciple:

You see this city? Here God lives among men, He will make His home among them; they shall be His people, and He will be their God; His name is God-with-them. He will wipe away all tears from their eyes; there will be no more death and no more mourning or sadness. The world of the past has gone. Then the One sitting on the throne spoke: 'Now I am making the whole of creation new,' He said, 'Write this: that what I am saying is sure and will come true.' And then He said, 'It is already done. I am the Alpha and the Omega, the Beginning and the End. I will give water from the well of life free to anybody who is thirsty; it is the rightful inheritance of the one who proves victorious and I will be his God and he a son to me' (Rv 21:3-7).

FOOTNOTES

Introduction

1. W. Brugger & K. Baker: *Philosophical Dictionary* (Spokane, Washington: Gonzaga Univ. Press, 1972) p. 6.
2. M.J. Adler: *The Idea of Freedom* (Garden City, N.Y.: Doubleday and Co., 1958) p. 616.

Chapter One

1. Mircea Eliade: *The Sacred and the Profane* (N.Y.: Harper & Row, 1961), tr. by W.R. Trask, p. 70.
2. Cited by Max Picard: *The World of Silence* (Chicago: H. Regnery, 1952), p. 98.
3. *St. Symeon the New Theologian: Hymns of Divine Love*, tr. by G. A. Maloney, S.J. (Denville, N.J.: Dimension Books, 1975), p. 46.
4. Carl Jung: *Psychology and Religion* (London: Routledge & Kegan Paul, 1973), Vol. II, p. 45.
5. *Ibid.*, p. 113.
6. St. Irenaeus: *Adversus Haereses*, from: The Ante-Nicene Fathers; Vol. 1, ed. A. Roberts and J. Donaldson (Grand Rapids, Mich.: Eerdmans), Book IV, chr. 38, pp. 521-522.
7. Cf.: T. F. Torrance: *The Doctrine of Grace in the Apostolic Fathers* (Edinburgh: Oliver & Boyd, 1948) and Nelson Glueck: *Hesed in the Bible*, tr. by A. Gottschalk (Cincinnati: The Hebrew Union College Press, 1967) for an exposition of *aheb, hen, hanan*, and *hesed*.
8. Torrance, *op cit.*, pp. 13-18.
9. Cf.: Edmund J. Fortman, S.J.: *The Theology of Man and Grace: Commentary* (Milwaukee: The Bruce Publishing Company, 1966), pp. 54-80 where the editor gives selections from the writings of T.F. Torrance, Wm. Manson, F. Amiot, Ch. Baumgartner, S.J., P. Gregory Stevens, O.S. B. and L. Cerfaux.
10. R. Otto: *The Idea of the Holy*, tr. by J. W. Harvey (N.Y.: Oxford Univ. Press, 1958), pp. 12-30.
11. *A Treasure of Russian Spirituality*, ed. by G. P. Fedotov (Gloucester, Mass.: Peter Smith, 1969), pp. 175-176.

Chapter Two

1. Perry LeFebre: *Understandings of Man* (Philadelphia: The Westminster Press, 1966) p. 16.
2. Cf.: Thomas M. Garrett: "Manipulation and Mass Media," *The*

Manipulated Man (*The New Concilium,* ed. by F. Bockle) (N.Y.: Herder & Herder, 1971) pp. 54-62.

3. A. Koestler: *Darkness at Noon,* tr. Daphne Hardy (N.Y.: Modern Library, 1961).

4. H. Bergson: *The Two Sources of Morality and Religion,* tr. R. Ashley Andra and Cloudesley Brereton (Garden City, N.Y.: Doubleday, 1954).

5. Pierre Teilhard de Chardin: *The Phenomenon of Man,* (N.Y.: Harper & Row, 1965).

6. C. LaFarge: "Mickey Spillane and His Bloody Hammer," in *Mass Culture: The Popular Arts in America,* ed. by B. Rosenberg and D. M. White (The Free Press of Glencoe, 1957) p. 177.

7. P. LeFavre, *op. cit.,* p. 20.

8. Emil Brunner: *Man in Revolt* (London: Lutterworth Press, 1953) p. 98.

9. M. Martin: *Jesus Now* (N.Y.: E.P. Dutton & Co., Inc., 1973) pp. 5-20.

10. *Ibid.,* pp. 41-72.

11. *Ibid.,* pp. 73.

12. Cf.: H. Felder: *Jesus of Nazareth* (London: Geo. E. J. Coldwell Ltd., 1938) pp. 133-135.

13. Cf.: Rudolf Pesch: "Jesus, a Free Man," *Jesus Christ and Human Freedom* (*Concilium,* N.Y.: Herder & Herder, 1974) pp. 66-67.

14. F. Malmberg: *Uber den Gottmenschen* (Frieburg, 1960) pp. 45-46, cited by R. Pesch, *op. cit.,* p. 68.

15. G. Maloney, S.J.: *Bright Darknesses: Jesus-Lover of Mankind* (Denville, N.J.: Dimension Books, 1977) p. 127

16. Kahlil Gibran: *Sand and Foam* (N.Y.: A.A. Knopf, 1928) p. 84.

17. Cited by Otto Borchert: *The Original Jesus,* tr. by L. M. Stalker (N.Y.: The MacMillan Company, 1933) p. 173.

Chapter Three

1. F. Dostoevsky: *The Brothers Karamazov,* tr. by Constance Garnett (London: Wm. Heinemann, 1912) pp. 268-269.

2. Cf.: Francois Marty, S.J.: "La liberte, qu'est-ce-que c'est?" *Christus.* (1972, no. 75) p. 360.

3. Albert Camus: *The Fall* (N.Y.: Vintage Books: Random House, 1956) tr. by Justin O'Brien, p. 118.

4. George Montague: *The Living Thought of St. Paul.* (Milwaukee: The Bruce Publishing Co., 1966), p. 143.

5. Cf.: Leander Keck: "The Son Who Creates Freedom," *Jesus Christ and Human Freedom* (The New Concilium: N.Y.: Herder and Herder, 1974) p. 74.

6. Carlos Castaneda: *Journey to Ixtlan* (N.Y.: Simon and Schuster, 1972) pp. 108, 111.

7. Cf.: Joseph Thomas, S.J.: "Fin de l'esclavage," *Christus* (no. 75, 1972) p. 420.
8. See the list of unfreeing moods and tendencies given by Dietrich von Hildebrand: *Transformation in Christ* (Garden City, N.Y.: Image Books: Doubleday, 1963) pp. 205ff.
9. Cf.: G. Maloney, S.J.: *Nesting in the Rock: Finding the Father in Each Event* (Denville, N.J.: Dimension Books, 1977).
10. Romano Guardini is excellent on this point in his work: *Freedom, Grace and Destiny* (N.Y.: Pantheon Books, 1960) pp. 77ff.
11. *A Treasury of Kahlil Gibran,* ed. by Martin L. Wolf; tr. from the Arabic by A. R. Ferris (N.Y.: The Citadel Press, 1959) pp. 154-155.

Chapter Four

1. N. Berdyaev: *Slavery and Freedom,* tr. from the Russian by R.M. French (London: Geoffrey Bles: The Centenary Press, 1943) pp. 252-254.
2. For a thorough presentation of the concept of spirit in both the Old and New Testaments, cf.: John L. McKenzie: *Dictionary of the Bible* (Milwaukee: Bruce Publishing Co., 1965) pp. 840-845.
3. Dale Moody: *Spirit of the Living God* (Philadelphia: The Westminster Press, 1968) pp. 33-57.
4. Cf.: Hendrikus Berkhof: *The Doctrine of the Holy Spirit* (Richmond, Va.: John Knox Press, 1964) p. 26.
5. *Ibid.,* p. 27.
6. See G. Maloney, S.J.: *Man—The Divine Icon* (Pecos, N.M.: Dove Publications, 1973).
7. St. Irenaeus: *Adversus Haereses,* Bk. V, Ch. 6, 1, in *The Ante-Nicene Fathers,* Vol. 1; ed. A. Roberts and J. Donaldson (Grand Rapids, Mich.: Erdmans) pp. 531-532.
8. Cf.: N. Berdyaev: *Freedom and the Spirit,* tr. from the Russian by O.F. Clarke (London, Geoffrey Bles: The Centenary Press, 1935) pp. 117-157; P. Tillich: *Systematic Theology;* Vol. 3 (Chicago: Univ. of Chicago Press, 1963) pp. 245-274.
9. P. Tillich: *The Interpretation of History* (N.Y.: Charles Scribner's Sons, 1936) p. 26.
10. J. Haughey: *The Conspiracy of God, the Holy Spirit in Men* (Garden City, N.Y.: Doubleday and Company, 1973) p. 98.
11. P. Tillich: *The Protestant Era* (Chicago: Univ. of Chicago Press, abridged edition, paperback, 1957) p. 57.
12. See: G. A. Maloney: *The Breath of the Mystic* (Denville, N.J.: Dimension Books, 1974) pp. 141-160.
13. P. Tillich: *Theology of Culture* (N.Y.: Oxford University Press, 1959) p. 7.

14. C. Spicq: *Agape in the New Testament,* Vol. 2 (St. Louis: Herder and Herder, 1965) p. 272.
15. See: G. A. Maloney, S.J.: *The Cosmic Christ, from Paul to Teilhard* (N.Y.: Sheed and Ward, 1968) pp. 182-220.

Chapter Five

1. Dr. Marie von Franz: "On Group Psychology," *Quadrant,* no. 13 (Winter, 1973) p. 9.
2. C. G. Jung: *Four Archetypes,* tr. by RFC Hull, extracted from *Archetypes and the Collective Unconscious,* Vol. 9, part 1, of the *Collected Works* of C. J. Jung *Bollingen Series XX* (Princeton, N.J.: Princeton University Press, 1970) p. 131.
3. Evagrius: *On Eight Thoughts,* in Early Fathers from the Philokalia. Tr. by E. Kadloubovsky and G. Palmer (London: Faber and Faber, 1954) p. 110.
4. Cf.: G. Maloney, S.J.: *The Breath of the Mystic* (Denville, N.J.: Dimension Books, 1974) pp. 161-174; also: *Inward Stillness* (Denville, N.J.: Dimension Books, 1976) pp. 105-119.
5. Wm. Kraft: *A Psychology of Nothingness* (Philadelphia: Westminster Press, 1974) p. 28.
6. *Ibid.,* p. 104.
7. Thomas Merton: *The Climate of Monastic Prayer* (Spencer, Mass.: Cistercian Publications, 1968) p. 147.
8. G. Marcel: *Problematic Man,* tr. by Brian Thompson (N.Y. Herder & Herder, 1967) p. 55.
9. *Ibid.,* p. 100.
10. Paul Tillich uses this example in: *The Courage to Be* (New Haven: Yale University Press, 1952).
11. St. Symeon the New Theologian: *The Hymns of Divine Love,* tr. by G. A. Maloney, S.J. (Denville, N.J.: Dimension Books, 1975) pp. 143-144.
12. St. Gregory of Nyssa: *The Life of Moses,* PG 44, 398-400.

Chapter Six

1 William of St. Thierry: *On the Solitary Life,* cited by J. M. Dechanet: Yoga and God (St. Meinrad, Ind.: Abbey Press, 1975) pp. 10-11.
2. St. Gregory of Nyssa: *Beatitudes,* Sermon 3: PG. 44; 1228.
3 Cf. Lawrence LeShan: *You Can Fight For Your Life: Emotional Factors in the Causation of Cancer* (N.Y.: M. Evans, Inc., 1977).
4 Ira Progoff: *The Symbolic and the Real* (N.Y.: McGraw-Hill Book Co., 1963) pp. 69-75

5. Triton: *The Magic of Space, pp. 138-149, as cited by Jon Mundy: "On Fear," Spiritual Frontiers;* Vol. IV (Summer, 1972) No. 3, p. 171.

6. Karl Menninger: *Whatever Became of Sin?* (N.Y.: Hawthorn Books, 1973).

7. Paul Tillich: *The New Being* (N.Y.: C. Scribner's Sons, 1955) pp. 38-39.

8. Carl Jung: *Modern Man in Search of a Soul* (London: K. Paul, Trench & Trubner, 1933) p. 259.

9. Dr. Carl Rogers: "Learning to be Free," *Person to Person, the Problem of Being Human,* ed. C. Rogers, B. Stevens et al (N.Y.: Pocket Books, Simon & Schuster, Inc., 1971) p. 43.

10. This is the term used by the Christian magazines: *Spiritual Frontiers* and *Science of Mind* as well as the famous Christian healer, Agnes Sanford in: *The Healing Light* (St. Paul, Minn.: Macalester Park Publishing Co., 1947).

11. See G. A. Maloney, S.J.: *Russian Hesychasm* (The Hague: The Mouton Press, 1973).

12. I have written about some of these dangers in a pamphlet called: *TM and Christian Meditation* (Pecos, N.M.: Dove Publications, 1976).

13. Ira Progoff: *The Well and the Cathedral* (N.Y.: Dialogue House Library, 1971).

14. G. Maloney, S.J.: *Inward Stillness* (Denville, N.J.: Dimension Books, 1976) pp. 51-54; *TM Christian Meditation,* op cit., pp. 33-36.

15. Agnes Sanford: *The Healing Light,* op cit., p. 37.

16. This is clearly brought out in books by the late Kathryn Kuhlman such as: *I Believe in Miracles* (N.Y.: Pyramid Books, 1962) Agnes Sandord: *The Healing Light, op cit.,;* and *The Healing Gifts of the Spirit* (N.Y.: J. P. Lippincott Co., 1966); Fr. Francis MacNutt, O.P.: *Healing* (Notre Dama: Ave Maria Press, 1974); and his second volume: *The Power to Heal* (Notre Dame: Ave Maria Press, 1977) and Michael Scanlon: *Inner Healing* (Paramus, N.J.: Paulist Press, 1974).

17. Two excellent books on inner healing are: Michael Scanlon, T.O.R.: *Inner Healing,* cited above and Dennis and Matt Linn, S.J.: *Healing of Memories* (Paramus, N.J.: Paulist Press, 1974).

18. Karl Rahner: *On Prayer,* (N.Y.: Paulist Press, 1968) p. 15.

19. Agnes Sanford: *The Healing Light, op cit.,* p. 126.

Chapter Seven

1. St. Bernard: *The Works of Bernard of Clairvaux:* Treatises II (Washington, D.C.: Cistercian Publications, 1973) p. 93.

2. Cf.: *New Catholic Encyclopedia* (N.Y.: McGraw Hill, 1967) art.: "Asceticism," pp. 111-112.

3. Origen: In Jeremiam Proph., Homil. XIX, 7, cited by: Pascal P. Parente: *The Ascetical Life* (St. Louis: Herder Book Co., 1947) p. 186.
4. St. Gregory of Nyssa: *Ascetical Works,* tr. by V. W. Callaghan (Washington, D.C.: Catholic U. of Am. Press, 1967) p. 87.
5. St. John Chrysostom: *Homilia 90 in Evang. S. Matthaei.*
6. Edward E. Malone: *The Monk and the Martyr* (Washington, D.C.: Catholic U. of Am. Press, 1950) p. 100 ff.
7. *Christian Asceticism and Modern Man,* tr. by Walter Mitchell (N.Y.: Philosophical Library, 1955) p. 40 (The collection of articles was first published by Cerf Publications, Paris, under the title: *L'Ascese Chretienne et l'Homme Contemporain*).
8. Jacques Leclercq: *Christ and the Modern Conscience* (N.Y.: Sheed and Ward, 1962) tr. by R. Matthews, pp. 245-246.
9. Cf.: Michel Olphe-Galliard, S.J.: "La Purete de Coeur d'apres Cassien," in Revue d'Ascetique et de Mystique, 17th yr. (Toulouse, 1936) pp. 28-60.
10. John Cassian: *Institutions Cenobitiques* in *Sources Chretiennes,* Vol. 109 (Paris: Cerf, 1965) Bk. IV, 34-35.
11. Cf.: George A. Maloney, S.J.: *Russian Hesychasm* (The Hague: Mouton Press, 1973) p. 76.
12. Cf.: Irene Hausherr, S.J.: "L'origine de la theorie orientale des huit peches capitaux" in *Orientalia Christiana,* Vol. XXX, no 86 (Rome, 1933) pp. 164-175.
13. Cf.: G. Maloney, S.J.: *Russian Hesychasm, op. cit.,* pp. 78-82.
14. Cf.: G.A. Maloney, S.J., *The Breath of the Mystic* (Denville, N.J.: Dimension Bks., 1974) pp. 83-108.
15 Cf.: G.A. Maloney, S.J.: *Nesting in the Rock: Finding the Father in Each Event* (Denville, N.J.: Dimension Bks., 1977). This book deals with Divine Providence and abandonment of oneself to God's loving presence found in each event.
16. This is a term that Adrian Van Kaam uses in his: *In Search of Spiritual Identity* (Denville, N.J.: Dimension Bks., 1975) pp. 172-196.
17. Cf.: Teilhard de Chardin: *The Divine Milieu,* tr. by B. Wall (London and N.Y.: Wm. Collins Sons & Co. and Harper & Row, Publishers Inc., 1960) p. 21.
18. *Ibid.,* p. 23.

Chapter Eight

1. S. Kierkegaard: *The Sickness Unto Death* (Princeton, N.J.: Princeto Univ. Press, 1941) p. 29.

2. C. Rogers: *On Becoming a Person* (Boston: Houghton Mifflin Company, 1961) p. 171.

3. G. Maloney, S.J.: *The Breath of the Mystic* (Denville, N.J.: Dimension Books, 1974) p. 42.

4. Iris Murdoch: *The Unicorn* (N.Y.: The Viking Press, 1963) pp. 188-189.

5. James Baldwin: *The Fire Next Time* (N.Y.: Dial Press, 1963) p. 44.

6. By George A. Maloney, S.J., June, 1977.

7. G.K. Chesterton: *Orthodoxy* (N.Y.: John Lane Company, 1908) pp. 107-108.

8. On this point, cf: Diogenes Allen: *Finding Our Father* (Atlanta: John Knox Press, 1974) p. 63.

9. St. Cyril of Alexandria: *De recta fide at Theod.:* PG 76, 1177. In a similar text Cyril writes: "Therefore is He man, made like unto us, that we might also be like unto Him. . . . that we might be gods and sons," in: *In Joan.* XX, 17; PG 74, 700 B.

10. St. Cyril: *In Joan.* VI, 54; PG 73, 577-580.

11. St. Symeon the New Theologian: *Chapitres Theologiques, Gnostiques et Pratiques,* 2, 19; Vol. 51 of *Sources Chretiennes* (Paris: Cerf, 1961), p. 76.

12. Rollo May: *Love and Will* (N.Y.: W.W. Norton & Co., 1969) p. 290.

13. T. S. Eliot: "East Coker," *Four Quartets* (N.Y.: Harcourt, Brace, 1943) p. 15.

14. Teilhard de Chardin: *The Divine Milieu* (N.Y.: Harper & Bros., 1960), tr. by B. Wall, pp. 127-128.